GEORGE MASON

Reluctant Statesman

GEORGE MASON
Reluctant Statesman

By

ROBERT ALLEN RUTLAND

Foreword by Dumas Malone

Illustrations by Richard J. Stinely

LOUISIANA STATE UNIVERSITY PRESS
Baton Rouge and London

To
CURTIS P. NETTELS

Foreword

THAT the name of George Mason should be acclaimed throughout the Republic whose birth pangs he shared, and indeed throughout the free world, will be agreed, I believe, by all American historians. He was the author of the Virginia Declaration of Rights, which was adopted three weeks before the national Declaration of Independence; and in this he charted the rights of human beings much more fully than Jefferson did in the immortal but necessarily compressed paragraph in the more famous document. Of the contemporary impact of Mason's Declaration there can be no possible question. Draftsmen in other states drew upon it when they framed similar documents or inserted similar safeguards of individual liberties in their new constitutions. Universal in its appeal, it directly affected the French Declaration of the Rights of Man and the Citizen of 1789. In our own time it is echoed in the Declaration of Human Rights of the United Nations. Writing in his old age, Lafayette said: "The era of the American Revolution, which one can regard as the beginning of a new social order for the entire world, is, properly speaking, the era of declarations of rights." More than any other single American, except possibly Thomas Jefferson, whom in some sense he anticipated, George Mason may be regarded as the herald of this new era; and in our own age, when the rights of individual human beings are being challenged by totalitarianism around the world, men can still find inspiration in his noble words.

The fact that Jefferson rather than Mason became the major American symbol of individual freedom and personal rights is attributable to no difference between the two men in basic philosophy, but was owing rather to the subsequent course of events and the accidents of history. Mason was by no means a minor figure in his own time; besides the Declaration of Rights he was the main author of the Virginia Constitution of 1776; and, because of his recognized wisdom, he was constantly consulted by other leaders. But, partly because of health, partly because of family cares, partly because of temperament, he was, in Mr. Rutland's apt phrase, a reluctant statesman. At times other leading Virginians sought to escape the burdens and responsibilities of public service—Jefferson being a good example—but no one of them carried reluctance to the same degree as Mason, who loathed routine legislative tasks and had no stomach for any sort of political intrigue. Venturing from home and his family as little as possible, he did not often leave Virginia. Thus, even in his own time, circumstance made this man of universal mind more a local than a national figure. As the architect of the new government in his own commonwealth he had shown himself to be constructive, but in connection with the new federal Constitution his own deep convictions caused him to assume a negative role and even to seem obstructive. As a delegate to the Federal Convention, he declined to sign the document which emerged from those closed sessions in

Philadelphia; he opposed ratification in his own state and went down in defeat. His chief objection to the new frame of government was that it lacked the sort of guarantees of individual freedom which he had set forth in his Declaration of Rights; and also that it went further than was necessary toward centralization, thus endangering local rights and liberties. Opposition of the sort he symbolized had a positive result in the adoption of the first ten amendments to the Constitution—the national Bill of Rights—and to that extent his contemporaries recognized the validity of his position. The triumphant Federalists were not kind in their judgment of their opponents, however; even George Washington was cool toward his old friend and neighbor. Furthermore, Mason's objections to Hamiltonian consolidation gave him a black mark in the history the partisans of the first Secretary of the Treasury did so much to write. It should be noted that Jefferson likewise protested against the omission of a bill of rights from the Constitution and eventually offered similar objections to Hamilton's policy. But Jefferson lived to achieve vindication in his own election to the presidency, by which time Mason was long since dead.

In his own "country"—that is, Virginia—Mason was and remained an honored prophet. Indeed there were those, like the historian of the Virginia Convention of 1776, who regarded the Declaration of Rights as a loftier work than the Declaration of Independence, which was in considerable part a political manifesto, designed to justify a change in government. Comparisons of this sort, if not odious, are quite unnecessary, for the two documents breathe the same philosophy. But the later national pronouncement can be advantageously supplemented by the fuller state declaration, and in certain cases Mason's language may be preferred. A good example follows:

> That all men are by nature equally free and independent, and have certain inherent rights, . . . namely, the enjoy-

ment of life and liberty, with the means of acquiring and possessing property, and pursuing and obtaining happiness and safety.

The author of the Declaration of Independence, who claimed no originality for his production, had nothing but praise for the author of the Declaration of Rights. Jefferson described Mason as "a man of the first order of wisdom among those who acted on the theatre of the Revolution, of expansive mind, profound judgment, cogent in argument, learned in the lore of our former constitution, and earnest for the republican change on democratic principles." Mason, he said, was a man "of the first order of greatness."

The story of such a person cannot fail to be of wide, and should be of universal, interest. The purpose of this book is something more than to inscribe his name in larger letters on the list of eminent champions of individual freedom. It is also to make him live again as a human being. There is no need to anticipate here the human story which the author of this book tells so well, but I cannot refrain from pointing out that Mason provides a striking example of the spirit of *noblesse oblige,* for he was born to wealth and a privileged position, just as Jefferson was. Such men cannot be explained in terms of economic determinism. Every reader is entitled to find his own answer to the question, why this master of broad acres and scores of slaves laid supreme emphasis on man's freedom and found tyranny of all sorts abominable. It may be suggested, however, that the spirit of liberty appears in high places as well as low—that, in fact, it assumes its noblest form when most disinterested. Rarely has it appeared in nobler form than in George Mason.

DUMAS MALONE

University of Virginia

Introduction

THE Potomac River south of Washington alters its slow, south-easterly course to form a giant horseshoe whose open end looks toward Baltimore and Annapolis. The western toe of this horseshoe is five miles below Mount Vernon, where the Potomac is forced to curve around a club-shaped peninsula called Dogue's Neck that protrudes from the Virginia shore. A river bend at such a point carries unpredictable currents that can make sailing difficult and, in a high wind, dangerous.

On a late winter day in 1735 George Mason, the third of the name in his family, set out from the Maryland shore and headed for Dogue's Neck. He never reached it. The sudden squall that capsized his sailboat left Ann Thomson Mason a widow with three children, the eldest, named for his father, not yet ten years of age.

Thus was the fourth George Mason plunged into an early

maturity. If the prospects for his future were brightened by in-
herited wealth, he nevertheless was to find the pursuit of happiness the most wearying quest of a life destined to end in a cloud
of frustration. Mason had the gout, a form of arthritis that re-
sponded in predictable fashion to the purges, poultices, and bloodletting that then marked the limit of medical progress. At Gunston
Hall, the home he built on Dogue's Neck, Mason discovered that
the management of plantation activities and the pleasures of
solitary study were an alternating current of bustle and quiet that
proved to be his gentlest, and most desirable, therapy.

If satisfaction in good works can also be a diversion from pain,
Mason found frequent and practical relief in the display of his
massive intellect. The Revolution showed its firebrand orator in
Patrick Henry, its confident leader of men in George Washington,
but it was Mason who was the dean of the intellectual rebels in
Virginia. The directness, the scholarly validity of his arguments
belied the fact that he was not a lawyer. Logic born of a love
affair with the classics gripped his mind when confusion seized
others. Demagoguery was his chief irritant, integrity his pallia-
tive. Burgesses and public officials showed how they coveted his
advice by continually approaching him for it. By preference he
was an informal statesman, except on rare occasions when only
by becoming an elected delegate could he make the weight of his
ability count heaviest.

In the labor pangs of its birth, the nation itself found Mason
a sympathetic and skillful attendant. While the concept of the
colonies uniting in a common cause was still formless and undirected, Virginians turned to him to diagnose the philosophical
tone of the developing revolution. Like other Americans born
into the Enlightenment (the cheerful eighteenth-century philosophy that proclaimed the perfectibility of man through reason and
experience), they believed in the British Constitution as the guard-
ian of their natural rights. But that unwritten constitution was a

matter of custom, not of record. Asked to spell out those rights so that in the future there would be no fruitless appeal to unwritten custom, Mason's answer was the Virginia Declaration of Rights.

Therein rests the keystone of his reputation, for that declaration led eventually to the first ten amendments—the Bill of Rights —of the American Constitution.

Today George Mason is vaguely remembered as the original architect of the American Bill of Rights so widely copied by new nations emerging into independence. His other contributions are less easy to measure. The days of Mason's years covered two-thirds of the eighteenth century. One of the first names the youngster heard was that of the benign English governor in Williamsburg, Colonel William Gooch. One of the last he was to hear in 1792 was that of his old friend and neighbor, George Washington. His years produced a mighty generation of Virginians, planter-statesmen whose way of life enabled them to tailor a philosophical idea to the practical fact of revolution. For the most part it was a process that took place slowly, subtly, almost daily, and without fanfare.

Mason remains as typical of that generation. History, in its concern with the Washingtons, the Jeffersons, and the Henrys, has swept most of his colleagues into the darkened corners of the eighteenth century. But history always seems to favor the man of action. In lively eighteenth-century America, and ever since for that matter, decisive events caught the fancy more readily than did monumental ideas. A single bullet whining across the Lexington common turned the most heated argument over colonial grievances into a skillful display of rhetoric.

An idea does not whine like a bullet. Born of contemplation, it is formless, undirected, of no meaning until it inspires an act. Then it is usually lost to sight. History encourages us to retain a mental image of the act. It can be visualized. But how does one visualize an idea?

George Mason was a producer of ideas who flourished at the time when leaders of the struggling former colonies were eager to experiment and to expand. Mason's ideas, placed on paper, drew the whole of the Revolution into focus. Soon they were read in Europe and drew the admiration of the men destined to guide France. "Life, liberty, and the pursuit of happiness" became the motto of the American Revolution, and the Bill of Rights its embodiment. No sooner would we drop the Bill of Rights from our form of government than we would ignore the antibiotics that make such a tragic joke of eighteenth-century medicine. Yet no one bothers much about who developed either.

When Mason articulated his ideas there were those who watched and listened and admired, and left ample evidence of their respect. With little more than a year remaining to him, Mason received a letter from one of them who wrote that "whenever I pass your road I shall do myself the honor of turning into it." It was the courtly kind of phrase Thomas Jefferson knew how to use, but our modern idiom offers nothing better. The road to Gunston Hall is an inviting one—a placid lane guarded by ranks of cedars and magnolias. Let us do ourselves the honor of turning into it for a visit with this towering Virginian.

Contents

ILLUSTRATIONS

GEORGE MASON
Reluctant Statesman

CHAPTER ONE

Heir to a Personal Dominion

Mention the Northern Neck to a present-day Virginian and there will arise in his mind the image of a long, flat finger of land still predominantly rural, still carrying landmarks left behind by a plantation aristocracy, still retaining in names like Westmoreland, Northumberland, and Lancaster reminders of Englishmen who settled there and established tiny outposts of British enterprise and culture. Three centuries ago those outposts flourished and multiplied against a background of tobacco. The soil of this slender peninsula was rich, its air was good, and its flanking rivers were nearby highways to Mother England.

Free of the swamplands and miasmatic "vapors" of watersheds farther to the south, the Northern Neck was a good place to settle down and build a home, to rear a family and make a fortune. Seventeenth- and eighteenth-century Virginians looked upon it as a hospitable wilderness and hoped to achieve those things. Once

3

there, they learned to live with and manipulate the cumbersome system by which the Neck slowly evolved from a proprietary dominion (by 1700 almost wholly controlled by the Fairfax family) into a pattern of plantations owned by aggressive, ambitious settlers. Absentee control by the Fairfaxes aided this transition. Entail, primogeniture, and artful techniques in speculation completed it and led to the accumulation of vast estates. "Headright" patents of land, which elsewhere divided huge tracts into small parcels, never caught hold on the Neck. Therefore the measure of a man became the number of square miles in his estate and the number of window panes in his mansion. The glass cost more than the land.

Most prosperous were the planters. And among those fortunate few, more successful than most, were the ancestors of George Mason. By the time he was born in 1725 the Mason name had become synonymous with wealth and leadership, talent and taste. Between the Potomac and Rappahannock rivers that flanked the Northern Neck there had sprung up an elite group of families. Their patriarchs were the leaders at the balls and the barbecues, the arbiters of justice in the courts. They owned the ferries, and they sat in the General Assembly. They were the Carters, the Lees, the Washingtons, the Masons.

From the very beginning, these families imparted to the Northern Neck a tinge of aristocracy that obscured the New World roots of the region. With land the basis for their wealth, it was the English model of elegance that was constantly portrayed as their ideal. It was the one they knew best. Few residents of the Neck would have called themselves Americans. When they thought of it at all, they probably thought of themselves as English-Americans, or simply as Virginians.

Born to the membership of gentlemen in this pleasant countryside, George Mason knew where to find the deer in its forests, the fish in its ponds and streams. Like the young colts he raced over the meadows toward a neighboring plantation, he was eager, exploratory, active, more active than he would ever again be, once his body had stopped growing and the yet-unsuspected gout had taken hold. To other second- and third-generation gentry he made himself an amiable companion. There would be plenty of time for them to step forward as the leaders of their class. The pattern had already been fixed, and before them were notable examples of the pathway to affluence and power.

Of these examples none was more impressive than that left by Robert ("King") Carter. When Carter died, in Mason's seventh year, he had acquired more than 200,000 acres of the Neck and had sat on the Governor's Council in Williamsburg. Men like Mason's father, and Augustine Washington, were either more modest or less speculative. They reasoned that between five and ten thousand acres would serve their needs temporarily. Their sons would discover such holdings adequate enough to launch them on their quest for the good life.

And good life it was for those landholders at the top rung of the Northern Neck's social ladder. Douglas Southall Freeman found eight distinct classes in pre-Revolutionary Virginia, running from the gentry to the slaves, with those two ranks both "supposed to be of immutable station." Between them stood small farmers, merchants, seafaring men, frontiersmen, servants, and convicts. Shifts in station could sometimes blur the social distinction between these middle classes; but if the rich did not get richer and the poor much poorer, at least they rarely swapped places. By Mason's time the main route to riches was by inheritance—the passing from father to son of immense estates. It was not yet the age of the self-made man, though symptoms of the acquisitive itch for land were still to be seen.

Out of land ownership, which fixed a man's place in this world of George Mason's, grew a kind of pastoral aristocracy. "Like one of the patriarchs, I have my flocks and my herds, my bond-men

and bond-women, and every soart of trade amongst my own servants, so that I live in a kind of independence on every one but
Providence." So boasted one Virginian early in the eighteenth
century. Rich loam and its "exquisite weed" was the keystone of
William Byrd's personal dominion, and of the larger one called
the colony of Virginia.

Tobacco, or notes representing tobacco, paid the bills abroad.
Thousands of broad, brown leaves were pressed into the huge
hogsheads that English merchants then jammed into their warehouses. Colorful damasks, silver plate, and choice Madeira came
up the rivers during the good years. Smaller orders and overdue
bills marked the lean ones. But year in and year out, tobacco supported the parson, paid the tax-gatherer, and entertained the royal
governor. Seasoned travelers looked at the good life based on its
cultivation and were reminded of the great English estates. The
planters were "much the same as about London," they said,
"which they esteem their home."

Yet tobacco, by 1725, was beginning to slip. Depressed prices,
worn-out acres, and sharp practices by both planters and merchants rudely jolted the complacency of the Northern Neck. Inspection acts to insure standards of quality and weight helped to
stabilize the trade though they could not postpone the end of the
tobacco tyranny in Tidewater agriculture. Mason's life spanned
the decline and fall of the system, and only prudent management,
developing with his responsibilities, set him apart from many of
his debt-enmeshed neighbors. Marked for early maturity through
his father's untimely death, Mason never forgot that it was better
to be due a pound than to owe a shilling.

Some of this prudence came directly from his mother. A
strong-willed woman with a widow's concern for her growing
children, she picked tutors to train her eldest son but did no
small amount of drilling herself. As an aide in making decisions

concerning the boy she enlisted John Mercer, Mason's uncle and a highly respected lawyer. It was a happy alliance. Good libraries were rare in the colony, and at Marlborough, a few miles down river from Dogue's Neck, Mercer owned one of the best. Book collector as well as lawyer, Mercer introduced the lad to shelves that held hundreds of the classics and almost every important legal treatise of the time, ranging from Coke's commentaries on Littleton to Mercer's own abridgment of the laws of Virginia. One volume that had cost his uncle five shillings must have made an impression, for it offered advice that Mason eagerly absorbed. Until he had his own copy, this edition of *Every Man His Own Lawyer* would do.

Days spent becalmed in the heady latitudes of Marlborough were not uninterrupted by outside diversion. To judge good horseflesh and "ride with a good saddle" were exterior signs of the gentleman, essential accomplishments. So was the curriculum of the race track, where the fortunes of some of his friends were either depleted or transferred. Mason could spot a good quarter horse and would occasionally back his judgment with a bet—a small one. There was risk enough in the fluctuating prices of tobacco and wheat; if he forgot that fact, his widowed mother reminded him.

Because he never enrolled as a student at the College of William and Mary he missed the chance to practice dancing as it was taught there. Yet he must have known the proper art, the way to take a lady's hand, to execute a turn. Had not the good Governor Gooch declared that there was "not an ill dancer in my government"? Fencing was also taught, though it was a social adornment better suited to the European nobleman than to the Virginia gentleman. Instruction seldom graduated to the more complicated positions and parries.

A good horseman, a fair dancer, an indifferent fencer: they were skills rated in that order by men of good breeding. By his twenty-first birthday in 1746, Mason was, by all the standards laid down for him and his peers, well-bred. Well-proportioned, too, even handsome under the wig that hid his brown hair. Clean-shaven in the manner of the times, his face was pleasantly round-shaped, no hint of mystery there except for a shaded, rugged look around the lower jaws. His eyes: hazel brown, with strongly curving, bushy eyebrows that might better have fitted a face leaner and less full.

There was, in truth, little about Mason's appearance at twenty-one to suggest his character. His scholarly bent was not reflected by a squint at the corners of his eyes; no lines yet appeared on his forehead to witness his defense against personal pain, his concern for the sorrowful state of affairs between England and her colonial subjects. Among friends, dressed in his London small-clothes, fashionable stockings sporting fancy clocks, neatly polished buttons and buckles, he was respected, if not yet distinguished. There would be time for that. Now he was simply rich.

Mason's inheritance, on reaching his majority, included thousands of acres of choice farm land in Maryland and Virginia. To the west, still to be surveyed, lay more thousands of uncleared acres. The Northern Neck estate included a wide variety of utility houses and sheds, numerous slaves, livestock, tools, furnishings, and other personal property. Tobacco, in storage awaiting a higher price or deposited in London, was a respectable asset, even though debit balances for British goods probably offset it. There were also bills of exchange and scattered holdings of cash—all in all an ample beginning for a young planter.

Long aware that this day would come, Mason was prepared for the responsibility of management. He plunged into the business of running a plantation with an aggressiveness that eliminated any notion that hired stewards and clerks might handle the main business and leave him plenty of time for reading and leisure. At

ANN EILBECK MASON, *"taller than the middle size, and elegantly shaped,"* *soon after her marriage to George Mason in 1750.*

the end of a day in the fields, inspecting crops, riding fences, haggling with merchants over prices at the warehouses, Mason did find time for his leisure. Then he surrounded himself with books, his own and those from his uncle's library, and proceeded to educate himself in a manner that was characteristically intense. Along with the wealth of legal writing available to him, he pored over medical treatises, bound volumes of English magazines, Shakespeare's works, Rollin's *Ancient History,* Stith's *History of Virginia,* and reports of Parliamentary debates. Naturally perceptive, keen of intellect, Mason revealed an appetite for reading that was of the type satisfied only when sharpened; the turn of a page might bring forth an even fresher discovery than before. It was his distinctive intellectual curiosity that permitted him to keep pace with the best minds in Virginia during a period when men usually established themselves as leaders by the age of thirty.

Possessed of wealth, wit, and intellect, Mason now lacked but two qualifications to meet the measure of a true son of the Northern Neck. He was a bachelor, and apparently a nimble one, considering the eligible young ladies who visited at neighboring plantations. "Eligibility" was important. The history of the Northern Neck had already become the history of interlocking family enterprise. Happily, no embarrassing shortage of candidates narrowed young George's choice. Across the Potomac in Maryland his search ended on the plantation of Ann Eilbeck. The sixteen-year-old girl enraptured the bookish young planter, being (as he recalled) "elegantly shaped" with "her complexion remarkably fair and fresh." On April 4, 1750, Ann and George stood before the Reverend John Moncure to repeat their marriage vows and begin a romantic partnership that would last for twenty-three years, and much longer in Mason's heart.

Thus did the second half of the eighteenth century open propitiously for George Mason. With family ties now formed by the new bride at his side, he needed only one more item to make the world truly his oyster. That was a sturdy, elegant mansion for this remarkably fair lady and the children she would bear him. A proper home for a proper family would be the next order of business.

WILLIAM BUCKLAND, "carpenter & joiner," left England to practice his craft in the New World. In addition to Gunston Hall, examples of his skill may still be seen in other Virginia and Maryland homes. Buckland died shortly after he sat for this portrait.

CHAPTER TWO

A Proper Home

MASON could have built a larger house, but he planned Gunston Hall exactly as he was learning to approach most human endeavors—with moderation and thoroughness. The story-and-a-half brick house grew toward completion between 1755 and 1758, taking on an aspect that was solid rather than grand. From the outside it looked small, deceptively so, for in fact it was quite roomy; with Mason's ever-growing family, its planners needed to fill every nook and cranny with living space.

The supervising craftsman was an Englishman, barely turned twenty-one, who came to America indentured to Mason's younger brother in 1755. Thomson Mason, preparing to leave England after studying law, had signed William Buckland at his brother's bidding. Work on the foundations and walls was already in progress when this fledgling architect stepped ashore at Mason's landing. The basic plan had been in the owner's mind for many months, for it was an uncomplicated arrangement similar to a number of other homes in the area. But a man of Mason's wide interests and responsibilities could not be on the scene all the time. Young Buckland seems early to have gained his confidence and convinced the master of the estate that the right man had been picked for the job. No ordinary indentured servant, he had come to the colony as a skilled "carpenter and joiner" who commanded twenty pounds salary per annum.

That the two men got along so well is a tribute to Buckland's ability. His ideas—excellent ones, it turned out—had to be accommodated to those of his employer, for Mason was not the kind to give him a free hand. The Virginian was above all things a manager who liked to control his affairs down to the last detail. Mason insisted that the sand used in the mortar come either from wells or the "river shoar," and exterior work called for mortar of stronger composition than that for inside partition walls. He warned a friend to be equally careful in watching such details. "I wou'd by no means put any clay or loam in any of the mortar," he wrote, because it was not only a weak material but "it is very apt to nourish and harbour those pernicious little vermin the cockroaches . . . and this I assure you is no slight consideration; for I have seen some brick houses so infested with these devils that a man had better have lived in a barne than in one of them."

No vermin would inhabit his palace. He wanted Gunston Hall to be the kind of dwelling his wife and family deserved, and the kind that proper hospitality, in a hospitable age, demanded. That goal was in his mind as he went over the plans with Buckland, checked the seasoning of the timbers, the riving of the shingles, the cut of the Aquia Creek stone quoins that were to square off the corners of the building. When new fires tested the chimney drafts in the spring of '58, the result of months of planning, four years of labor, and hundreds of pounds sterling stood ready for its final inspection.

MASON'S ORIGINAL PLAN *for a traditional type of country home, with four rooms and a central hallway on the main floor, gave William Buckland ample room to practice his genius as a master woodcarver and joiner.*

TRADITIONAL SOUTHERN HOUSES *of the period had no end windows on the first floor. Mason's plan provided three small upper windows for extra ventilation in the bedrooms and an outside entry to the basement that permitted precious cargoes of claret and madeira to be moved directly to the wine cellar.*

THE CENTRAL HALLWAY.

THE PALLADIAN DRAWING ROOM.

Buckland had served his master well. Mason was enchanted by Buckland's skill as a woodcarver, and in that respect gave the Englishman free rein. Certainly the entire structure combined classic touches with original qualities of grace and form. Following the style of the day, the ceilings were high and the central passage wide, so that cool breezes could drift through on scorching August days. Between a double elliptical arch in the main hall Buckland carved a pineapple, the ancient symbol of hospitality. Gunston Hall was meant to be a place of welcome and conviviality, and Buckland's art caught his employer's intent.

Approaching Gunston Hall from the post road the visitor dismounted before the entrance porch where graceful Doric columns were paired on each side to support a Palladian archway. Inside, each doorway led into a room decorated with dentilled moldings and carved facings of incomparable beauty. The Chinese Chippendale room, used for dining, demonstrated Mason's willingness to let Buckland try the latest London designs then being acclaimed for their daring. But in the adjoining Palladian room Buckland's virtuosity was breath-taking: arched cupboards set into the walls were flanked by fluted pilasters and enclosed by broken pediments. The carving was superb in its detail and proportion. Here was the touch of a master craftsman, the taste, the sense of scale of an artist. Between chair rail and cornice, decorative fabric covered the pine sheathing of the walls. To play loo or drink Madeira in front of the elaborate fireplace might seem almost a desecration in a setting that, at the least, invited poetic declamations. But this was the drawing room, and it was for friends. Across the hall from the dining room was Mason's study, which also became an office for the more prosaic hours of business discussion. Beyond a narrow passage was the master bedroom.

For the nine Mason children who survived the rigors of infancy the half-story upstairs furnished ample room. Small fireplaces kept them comfortable in winter months, when the four giant chimneys sent skyward wisps of burning oak and ash. Five dormer windows on each side of the steep-pitched A-roof let in natural light for their playtime hours, and the six rooms were filled with many a mirthful sound while the master of the house read or talked or entertained downstairs.

For the rear porch Buckland drew on a pentagon-shaped plan with five exposed sides that framed a view of the boxwood gardens below and the Potomac River beyond. To the east a yardway adjoined the house. There, conveniently close for the hustling house servants at meal time, Buckland placed the kitchen and the wellhouse. Joined to the same side of the house was the bulkhead entrance to the basement and its cool storage for butter, milk, wines, and river-ice.

Mason's planning and Buckland's tools had shaped a house that would have honored Grosvenor Square, to say nothing of colonial Virginia. Never a man to feign modesty, the owner knew that the jewel of his eye was also one of the showplaces of the Neck—not grandiose, but in detail elegantly perfect: the characteristic of everything he undertook. And like most of the things George Mason constructed, Gunston Hall was built to last.

Ordinarily a man of sober judgment, Mason showed a sense of humor when he supervised the landscaping around his home. With a surveyor's precision and a knowledge of oblique perspective he planted about two hundred cherry trees in four rows, two on each side beginning about seventy-five yards from the front doorway. First-time visitors to Gunston Hall, who had arrived at night from either the post road or from the river landing below, would be led to the front entrance. With a twinkle in his eye Mason would ask, "How many trees do you see before you?" "Four," was the inevitable answer, whereupon Mason would lead the visitor to the side of the doorway and watch the optical illusion dissolve in "delight and surprise."

THE FAMOUS CHINESE CHIPPENDALE *dining room at Gunston Hall, where William Buckland created an American showpiece with scalloped crown mouldings and cornices reflecting the Oriental influence in colonial Virginia.*

MASON'S STUDY, *where the number of books was not as notable as the titles. Mason's native intellect as well as his reading habits impressed his contemporaries, who judged the master of Gunston Hall to be, as Jefferson said, "of the first order of greatness."*

THE RESTORED GARDENS *on the Potomac side of Gunston Hall have become a showplace of southern colonial horticulture since the late Louis Hertle gave the property to the people of Virginia. Opened to the public in 1952, the buildings and grounds are held in trust by the Colonial Dames of America and administered by a board of regents.*

AN ELEVATED GAZEBO-TYPE *of garden building stands between the main house and the slope where George and Ann Mason are buried. The English boxwood hedges are believed to be scions of the first varieties planted under Mason's direction.*

Beyond the mansion proper, Mason's estate took on the self-sufficient character of other colonial plantations. Separate small buildings each housed a different activity, from the ever-present Virginia smokehouse to the schoolhouse, spinning and weaving house, laundry, blacksmith shop, stables, barns, and "necessaries." In quarters for Mason's ninety slaves lived household servants as well as carpenters, coopers, tanners, field hands, sawyers, shoemakers, weavers, and a distiller, whose happy task it was to prepare persimmon brandies and applejack for storage beneath the solid planked flooring of Gunston Hall.

The plantation, including a deer park that delighted Mason's children, covered close to five thousand acres. A glimpse into Mason's method of personally operating these vast holdings comes from his son John's memoirs: "My father kept no steward or clerk about him. He kept his own books and superintended, with the assistance of a trusty slave or two, and occasionally of some of his sons, all the operations at or about" the estate. For his personal aide Mason relied heavily on James, an able mulatto slave. As his own field manager Mason kept most of his cultivated land planted in wheat, corn, or tobacco. The grains supplied staple items for the diets of every member of the plantation community. Tobacco was the chief money crop, furnishing a trade balance that brought the Masons "mail-order" goods from London.

All the evidence suggests that colonial Virginians imported large shipments of fine furniture, porcelain, damask coverings and draperies, printed silks and cottons, brocades, calf-bound books, silver flatware and plate, delicate glassware, jewelry, instruments, tools, and toys. The arrival of a ship from England carrying the master's order differed little in excitement from a modern Christmas morning when the shipping crates and barrels were unpacked. Orders sometimes took more than a year to fill, so plenty of surprises and some disappointments were inevitable. If items were substituted or shoddy goods came back for high-grade tobacco,

Virginians were inclined to hold the British merchants responsible for a "piece of villany somewhere."

This was George Mason's world, and he gave every evidence of believing it to be the best of all possible worlds. Nature and affluent forebears had created a life that would have made medieval barons envious. From the graceful simplicity of the Gunston Hall facade to the boxwood allée in the garden, all the signs were those of wealth, taste, and luxury. We may be sure that Mason's board was a match to any set on the Northern Neck, with no grand occasion needed to bring ham, roasts, game, puddings, fruits, fresh vegetables, tarts, wine, cider, milk, tea, coffee, and chocolate onto the groaning table. Travelers weary of jolting along the public highway knew the carved pineapple at Gunston Hall was no empty symbol. Neighbors found Mason equally gracious when they came calling to discuss tobacco prices, the lineage of a stud horse, or that favorite conversational topic: land.

Mason could look at his growing family, his increasing estates, and see the good things about him that called for a prayer of thanks as he and his family sat in his pews at Pohick Church, pews that cost him £ 14/11/8 each. Prayer book opened on his lap, Mason could ponder the scripture reading that declared, "For unto whomsoever much is given, of him shall be much required."

The duty thus charged meant to Mason serving his family, his church, and his neighbors. Like others of his generation he was ready to accept these responsibilities, at least those that did not involve office-seeking. The hard business of campaigning for office, with its back-slapping and communal cider-drinking, was not for him. If his neighbors really wanted him to serve that was something else, for they all shared a primary concern for keeping county and colonial affairs on an even keel. Gradually they came to recognize that if George Mason said something was so it probably was; and if he said it was not a good thing to support then they had better leave it alone.

With the management of plantation business that directly involved the welfare of more than one hundred people, Mason combined, in the less demanding hours of the day, his passion for reading and study. The result was a quality of balance in his preparation for leadership that might have been less soundly developed had he spent his youthful years attending college or reading for the bar. Possessing no formal law training, never licensed to practice or admitted to the bar, he still was often mistaken for a lawyer. His advice on legal matters was eagerly sought and willingly given. There is evidence that contentious neighbors dropped their truculence when threatened by a legal bout with, as one admitted, "an adversary so potent in mind . . . as Col. G. Mason."

The law had two complementary appeals for Mason. While it was an intellectual pursuit, it was also a business necessity. A man needed more than a passing knowledge of it if he was to protect and add to his investments, particularly in land. Successful speculating and trading in land, the basis of colonial wealth, required an intimate acquaintance with the ins and outs of titles and charters. Both were often in a mess. The man with the most convincing precedents and evidence was the man who walked out of court with a favorable verdict in his pocket.

Mason's holdings on the Northern Neck and to the west (into the Kentucky country) increased throughout his lifetime, eventually to reach more than 75,000 acres. In addition, he became deeply involved in the Ohio Company scheme along with other prominent Virginians seeking gains through western land speculation. Before the complex problem was finally tossed into the lap of His Majesty's court in London, Mason had probed the colonial laws and charters for every scrap of evidence to support the Virginia claim to some 500,000 acres.

These activities caused Mason to study colonial land laws with a thoroughness his contemporaries were quick to admire. His petitions to the Governor and Council of Virginia in support of claims regarding headright certificates (legal titles issued to persons who brought immigrants to the colony, with fifty acres granted for each "head") which he bought on speculation were as masterful as any lawyer might have drafted. Mason became the expert consultant in that field; and revolutionary legislators accepted his opinion as possibly the final word in land matters.

A different course of legal training for Mason was given by the county court. Before he was thirty the young planter began serving as a justice of the peace in Fairfax County. This was the most important of the local appointive offices a gentleman might hold, for it was practically a lifetime job with a broad range of duties. Not only did the justice settle minor suits, issue peace bonds, and send out court orders; he also sat with the other justices of the county in the important monthly "court days." The whole spectrum of civil and criminal cases passed before the assembled justices. They approved road building and other public works, levied taxes, called elections, and made the county's laws. They could revoke the license of a slovenly tavern operator; they kept a watchful eye on the public scales at county tobacco warehouses. Orphans, bastards, and slaves fell under their charge. In short, they held tremendous local powers that could touch every man's affairs.

Many justices, and Mason was one, frequently left off their duties on the court merely to assume other public concerns as members of the parish vestry, where they supervised indentures, placed apprentices, and provided for the destitute. Little took place throughout the countryside that escaped the attention of a vestryman-justice. He often knew his neighbors better than they knew each other, a fact that served him well when they became constituents and he their voice.

That Mason could manage his own plantation in addition to his responsibilities as both justice and vestryman seems sufficient evidence of his energy. But in 1754 he accepted a trusteeship for the town of Alexandria, taking on a new set of duties for the rising town akin to those he already performed as a county justice. When to these obligations were added those of service in the militia company and in the colonial assembly, the accumulated burden of public service began to grow too heavy. Mason was to become more and more aware of this.

A brief taste of life as a burgess in 1759-1760 surfeited him. However pleasant Williamsburg might have been during the session, other factors convinced him that further service there was out of the question. The private exchanges of influence that came later to be known as logrolling, and the time-consuming, often pointless oratory seemed to him an alliance of irresponsibility and stupidity. Supervision of the commonweal certainly appeared to generate a lot of nonsense. Affairs outside his county, he therefore concluded, could be left to others, provided the leadership was forthcoming. If it were not, he found that it might take an indirect route through advice to friends, thus sparing him the tedium of a long legislative session and tiresome journeys between Gunston Hall and Williamsburg.

The press of business at Gunston Hall or the discomforts of travel were mere minor impediments to public service when compared to Mason's fluctuating state of health. Indeed, health was a subject that few of those at Gunston Hall, or elsewhere, were able to forget for long. Busy parsons, funeral processions, and long lines of mourners were frequent and tragic reminders of the shortness of life. Infant mortality rates were so high that burial plots seemed reserved for the innocent. The mother who had borne five or six children and still breathed was almost living a charmed life. A prudent man prepared a will before his twenty-fifth birthday. At age forty, he was old.

How could it have been otherwise? The most learned doctors

had no knowledge of bacteriology and remained convinced that night vapors and miasma carried many of the death-dealing sicknesses that tortured their patients' bodies. Hippocrates' observations from ancient days were still the basis of much medical practice. The learned Dr. Boerhaave simply modified the early doctrine of the body humors as health controls—phlegm, black bile, yellow bile, and blood—and held that disease resulted from the faulty interaction of these elements. Diet and the humors went hand in hand. Bad blood was the characteristic of the ill, and a combination of nostrums for internal use and bloodletting (phlebotomy) became basic to much eighteenth-century therapy.

Mason, not unlike his fellow Americans, accepted this medical knowledge as the best obtainable. Trained doctors, when available, depended to a large degree upon trial-and-error medication. When sickness struck, the natural recourse was to the pages of such a work as Boerhaave's *Aphorisms*, which described the symptoms and prescribed remedies.

Gout was Mason's constant foe. An old affliction of mankind, this particular form of arthritis was no stranger to a succession of Mason households. Its hereditary grip fastened itself upon the master of Gunston Hall while he was still in his thirties. So weakened was he by one early attack that for days he limped about on crutches and had to be carried from place to place in a chair. It was the beginning of an exhausting struggle against an insidious enemy.

In Mason's day gout was considered a distemper that might have as its cause either obscure hereditary factors or an imbalance of the humors. For some sufferers there was at least the consolation that gout usually attacked "men of acute and deep sense, that exercise the same much, and protract their studies late in the night." But all authorities agreed that once victimized by gout, a person was "hardly ever free from some pain" thereafter. Boerhaave declared a complete cure was impossible, and held that hereditary gout (as opposed to that contracted from overindulgence or venery, where temperance could intercede) was "the most difficult of all to cure, or even to ease."

Mason was not impressed, when the Earl of Chatham became a hero to Americans, that this great Briton also suffered excruciatingly from gout while he remained a steadfast public servant. Gout was rather Mason's overworked excuse from public service. When he consoled his daughter on the loss of an infant, who had thus missed a life of misery, it must have been with some tinge of personal remorse. Yet Mason, like Shakespeare, would have agreed that

> One that's sick o' the *gout,* had rather
> Groan so in perplexity than be cur'd
> By the sure physician death.

But the suggested treatments of the day raised the serious question whether the disease or the cure was more to be dreaded.

Dr. Boerhaave, whose *Aphorisms* may have been the mainstay of Mason's own library, believed that a good deal of the misery of gout could be relieved by inducing the bad blood in the joints to move to other parts of the body. To do this, he urged relief by "suction, friction, plaisters, and blisters, fomentations, bathings, issues, setons, and strong purges." When gout "turned inwards" to attack the brain, lungs, pleura, or abdomen, the best advice was to

> immediately apply large blisters to the thighs; to the parts that used to ake; apply lukewarm salt, aromatick fomentations; let him be bid to walk hard, or be galopp'd stoutly in a chaise; let him take a large quantity of some sudorific aromatic drink, or, if that will not do, of old Rhenish wine

with all of this followed by "a warm bed and sweat."

Being a reasonable man, Mason probably drew the line at

chaise-galloping. But it is quite likely that he suffered through the recommendation for "whipping the [afflicted] part with nettles" to create a counterirritant. Another device was "a match or actual fire held at a distance till you raise a large blister, which must be cut to let out the matter." Mason readily accepted bleeding as part of the treatment for sporadic attacks of gout, as it left "the patient betwixt the fits entirely free, and his joints unhurt."

Bloodletting was such a universal remedy that we may question whether doctors or butchers spilled the most. In theories of the day bleeding reduced the volume of bilious fluids in the body and prevented the obstruction of matter in the narrow blood vessels. This was supposed to relieve those inflammations that might accompany gout, and in Mason's case definitely were present. He complained of gout in his joints and stomach and of St. Anthony's fire (erysipelas) on his skin. Nothing like a little bloodletting to gain relief, Mason agreed, and he urged his children when ill to follow the same course.

This incurable malady had its obvious effect on his personality. Considering the misery involved in a carriage ride that relayed every bump to his bones, the five-day trip to Williamsburg had nightmarish aspects for Mason. At home, when four or five youngsters moved on tiptoes upstairs it was seldom that Father, sitting below in the study with his tender feet propped on pillows, was in high spirits. Small wonder that his children remembered him as a kind but decidedly firm gentleman. Those outside the family could be a little more frank. George Mason, a charming host on his good days, could be quite a grouch on his bad ones.

Ill health then was a dominant theme in Mason's life after his thirtieth birthday. If it made him at times a hypochondriac it also furnished him with a convenient reason to avoid bothersome duties, and allusions to him were apt to be qualified by "if Colo. Mason is well enough." Certainly he showed up often at the apothecary shops in Williamsburg and Dumfries, where he could store up nostrums in quantity. Calomel, mercuris dulcis, and ginseng were high on his list of remedies. Ginseng was believed in that day, as a fellow Virginian noted, to dissolve "all phlegmatic and viscous humors, that are apt to obstruct the narrow channels of the nerves." What could be better for gout?

Crippled and in pain from time to time, Mason passed from youth into middle age as a man of business, a clear thinker, and a normally friendly neighbor. He was not a hail-fellow-well-met sort of man. All the signs indicate that he was as dignified at the race track as in the family pews. Mix with dignity Mason's frequent spells of the gout and the long hours spent in a sick bed, and some of his outbursts of impatience and short temper are explained if not excused. The few surviving anecdotes telling of his humor reveal that it was sarcastic rather than light-hearted. In his total makeup, George Mason probably frowned as much as he smiled.

But if sickness caused Mason to be essentially humorless, his physical activity was only partially impaired, his mental agility not at all. When he reached his fortieth year in 1765 he was thoroughly entrenched as one of the leading men of the Northern Neck. One finger always on the pulse of local affairs, he coveted not a single honor beyond those he already held. Let the Lees, the Washingtons, and others take over the affairs of the Colony if they wished. For Mason it was a time of quiet in his life, for happy hours and comfortable living at Gunston Hall, for rearing his children in a proper manner, and for gradual retirement from political business altogether.

All this might have been, had there been no Stamp Act.

CHAPTER THREE

"The Necessity of the Times"

HISTORICAL "ifs" are guesswork, therefore useful only when they set off a fact more clearly by focusing on its opposite. If there had been no Stamp Act the rupture between England and America might only have been postponed. The Stamp Act was a fact that Americans had to face, and it touched off a long series of incidents that reached a climax on the Lexington green. Yet if the British had not tinkered with the old colonial system, George Mason might have lived out his days as a gentleman planter, taking only occasional notice of colonial politics. But the tinkering began. As clumsy men often do, the British leaders stepped on so many toes that instead of isolated outcries they soon had to face the wrath of thirteen colonies. After the year 1763, British policy leaped from crisis to crisis, generating colonial unity in a way that would have seemed incredible a few years earlier.

No matter how Boston radicals may have welcomed the friction with England, Mason and most other Virginians did not. So the peaceful days prior to 1763 were soon a precious memory, replaced on the one hand by growing American talk about self-rule and on the other by determined ministers in London who shook with rage at American impertinence.

It all began innocently enough. British officials, failing to see that they were in fact sharply reversing old policies, had sought new sources of tax revenue. To the colonial American, Mother England seemed suddenly to have turned into a grasping and greedy scold. Moreover, colonial pocketbooks that had been reasonably obese became flabby, convincing Americans that the shift in policy, far from being shrewd statesmanship, was merely common, ordinary rapacity.

The Stamp Act was the first symbol of the power struggle. In Virginia Patrick Henry and Richard Henry Lee were the foremost spokesmen of resistance. Henry supplied the fiery oratory while Lee represented the rising element that in a decade would be called the radical patriot group. If these two men occupied the center of the stage, Mason was close by in the wings, or often in the prompter's box. During the opening scenes of this developing drama he became a close friend of Lee and may have been the coadjutor when Lee wrote a bold address to Governor Fauquier in 1765.

Specie-poor Virginians, having passed a paper currency act that British ministers promptly struck down, complained that Americans had the right to be governed by "laws made with our own consent." A copy of the address in Mason's handwriting further declared that Americans gloried in their British connection "as our only security; but this is not the dependance of a people subjugated by the victorious arms of a conquerer."

The stamp tax that soon followed quickly raised American hackles. Coming on the heels of the Currency Act, it was to men of Mason's circle a clear case of an illegal levy that had to be re-

PATRICK HENRY, *the volatile Virginian whose enormous popularity made him the first governor of the new state of Virginia.*

sisted. He actively joined the patriots by drafting a plan for the Fairfax County burgesses that would permit certain classes of debtors and landlords to sidestep the use of stamped paper. Then abruptly the whole stamp dispute took an embarrassing personal turn for Mason. His naive cousin, George Mercer, appeared in the Colony as His Majesty's duly-appointed stamp distributor. In Williamsburg he received the kind of acclaim reserved for the bearers of plague. The reception committee, wrote Governor Fauquier, could have been called a mob "did I not know that it was chiefly if not altogether composed of gentlemen of property in the colony."

Violence averted, Mercer beat a meek retreat to England. There he and others assured Englishmen of the lengths to which Americans would go to resist such taxes, but fresh news of threats to suspend American imports of English goods drew more attention. Parliament, becoming jittery about the whole business, accepted the advice of frightened British merchants and repealed the odious act, fearing the bankruptcy of twenty London firms much more than a thousand protests from the colonies.

News of the quick reversal by Parliament brought rejoicing in Virginia, as it did in the other colonies. Though the face-saving Declaratory Act, a companion piece of legislation, held that Parliament still had the right to legislate for the colonies in "all cases whatsoever" the Americans put their emphasis on the measure that revoked the stamp tax.

Mason, keenly conscious of the two interpretations, knew that questions of imperial rule had not been settled. When a group of London merchants admonished the colonists for their spirited resistance to a lawful measure Mason testily denied the implications of treason. His open letter to British businessmen, addressed to the *London Public Ledger* in the spring of 1766 and signed "A Virginia Planter," showed deep concern for strained British-American relations.

Americans were tired of being treated as a schoolmaster would handle unruly boys, Mason insisted. The repealed Stamp Act dealt with a single grievance, and had not wiped out remaining sources of friction such as the enforcement of the British Navigation Acts. (Many of those statutes, aimed at insuring a healthy trade for the empire, had long gathered dust. Recent tightening of them hampered open smuggling that had gone on for years, proved a boon to informers, and encouraged eager Crown agents to flout trial by jury and due process of law in their search for personal gain.) Technically, an American could still be dragged "a thousand miles from his own country" and tried before a judge whose income might depend upon conviction. These evils grew out of British efforts to monopolize American trade, Mason explained, even though this prosperous commerce already rested to a degree on a precarious credit system. Certain British ministers, disregarding this economic tie or misjudging its importance, might try some other scheme as distasteful as the Stamp Act. All the old wounds would then instantly reopen.

Mason warned the British that compulsion could not sustain a favorable British-American trade balance. A growing America, nurtured on free principles, would not accept oppression after having once "tasted the sweets of liberty." Another Stamp Act, or anything approaching it, "would produce a general revolt in America." These harsh words, he added, came not from a hotheaded radical but from a semi-retired farmer who "has seldom meddled in public affairs, who enjoys a moderate but independent fortune . . . who adores the wisdom and happiness of the British Constitution." Moreover, the spirit of resistance to oppressive British measures gripped "nine-tenths of the people who have been so basely misrepresented to you, and whom you would lately have treated as rebels and outlaws."

The letter tells us a good deal about Mason. The tone was defiant, and the defiance was aimed at the purses of the merchants, where he knew the British to be most vulnerable. By comparing Parliamentary laws to edicts from a "Turkish divan," Mason justified resistance and even risked being called an outlaw. Concern over an Englishman's basic rights led him to call for their preservation along the Potomac as well as beside the Thames. It was a logical, if argumentative, document.

England was in no mood to heed preaching from America. The Revenue Act of 1767 proved that she was committed to a course of pressure on America, pressure that could be relieved only by compliance. Bold men from Massachusetts southward assumed leadership, announcing bluntly that they would never kiss the rod that flayed their backs. The arrival of British troops in Boston in 1768 revealed the steps London was prepared to take. A grim prospect faced Bostonians: regulations backed with bayonets.

Clumsily handling the revenue problem as though they were dealing with country bumpkins, the British found too late that their distant cousins were serious, proud, and ready to risk everything. From his observation post at Gunston Hall, Mason sidestepped the specious argument about Great Britain's right to regulate for trade but not for revenue. The Townshend duties on exports to America were money-raising measures, and to accept them (so the patriots urged) would mark the beginning of the end for free colonial government. Equally obnoxious were the provisions for writs of assistance meant to tighten enforcement of the laws and end the dangerous but profitable smuggling trade along the American coast. Mason looked upon these acts, if allowed to stand, as the death-knell of colonial rights.

Following the Boston vanguard, the Virginians chose as their weapon a stringent boycott on taxed British goods. Although not a member of the House of Burgesses, Mason knew the temper of his region. He drafted a set of Non-Importation Resolves, perhaps at Washington's bidding, and the master of Mount Vernon carried them to Williamsburg. When Washington introduced them in the House they were intended to be the heart of the plan adopted by the patriot group. Governor Botetourt denied the burgesses the right to approve the resolves and dissolved their session, but they promptly moved to the Raleigh Tavern and voted in favor of the "Non-importation resolutions of the Association at Williamsburg."

Mason's plan was an altered version of the northern schemes, "adapted to our circumstances," he had explained to Washington. It called for plain living and stressed the basis for colonial harmony: American raw materials in exchange for British manufactured goods. The final version was weaker than Mason had proposed, as the delegates rejected his suggestion that they refrain from exporting tobacco to England until their grievances were redressed. But the heart of his plan, to keep pressure on the British merchants, remained.

As the association was voluntary, public opinion admittedly was to be the enforcing element that would keep in line timid Virginians who through habit avoided political quarrels. If patriotic appeals would not keep British goods out of a pantry, then shame might do the trick. Mason emphasized this as the patriot's weapon, and his hard-fisted attitude showed that his semi-retirement only masked a vigorous personal opposition to British measures. He urged friends to shun violators of the boycott in public; "they should be loaded with every mark of infamy and reproach." Mason wanted the list of violators published in the *Virginia Gazette* and elsewhere so that each man might be known as an enemy of the people. Watchdog committees were to seek out the fainthearted, he added, and those selected for service had to be the most respectable men in the country if the plan were to carry its full weight.

A partial repeal of the Townshend duties gave the colonies another breathing spell, but Mason reviewed the record with misgivings. The boycott had not been carefully observed in Virginia

GEORGE WASHINGTON. *A member of the Virginia House of Burgesses for sixteen years before the Revolution, he knew something of the internal politics, as well as the tactics, of war.*

by some, and he feared that the British might interpret disaffection as a sign of fundamental weakness. A substantial group of men had no stomach for open quarrels. The respected Robert Carter Nicholas spoke for a powerful segment of the colony when he declared, "Let things but return to their old channel, and all will be well; we shall once more be a happy people." Perplexed by the stubborn policy of the British ministers, Mason seriously doubted that they had any notion of allowing the colonies to resume their comfortable station in the imperial orbit.

In March, 1773, Mason's speculations on future British policy were interrupted by a staggering blow. His wife Ann, "after a painful and tedious illness of more than nine months," died of a malady that he could describe in terms no more specific than "a slow fever." "Formed for domestic happiness, without one jarring atom in her frame! Her irreparable loss I do and ever shall deplore," he sadly recorded in the family Bible.

Taking stock of his personal life, Mason felt the full weight of his forty-eight years, and while the earth was still fresh on Ann's grave he despondently wrote a will. The long mourning period began. Sounds of childish gaiety in the rooms of Gunston Hall gave way to an ordered and respectful quiet, both upstairs and down. To force his attention on other matters Mason applied himself to an extensive study of the colonial land laws in an effort to buttress Virginia claims to the great Northwestern territory.

In December the shock of the Boston Tea Party, which ruffled the calm of most American households, helped to bring Mason out of mourning. The retaliatory Boston Port Bill, making the New England metropolis a kind of armed camp, was alarming enough to unify colonial thought on resistance measures.

At this critical juncture Mason made one of his infrequent trips to Williamsburg on pressing personal business. Settling down at an inn he promptly saw that his own problems were less pressing than those described to him by burgesses who sought him out, eager to listen to his reactions and to enlist his aid in arousing Virginians to the common danger. Here Mason met Patrick Henry for the first time and judged the incomparable orator to be "the first man upon this continent, as well in abilities as public virtue." A general call for prayer and fasting came from the delegates as they tied their fortunes to those of beleaguered Boston. In an effort to salvage his own western land claims from the chaos that had hit Virginia speculators, Mason stayed in Williamsburg but urged his family to pay strict attention to the call for mourning dress and to attend the prayer meeting held for their brethren in Boston.

The feeling that was running so high in Williamsburg must have impressed him. He returned to Gunston Hall an even firmer patriot than when he had left it a few weeks before. Obviously his warning that colonists would not be treated as schoolboys affected Parliament no more than a mild dew affects the Thames River. The British master believed in the rod as the proper medicine for upstarts. That was the now-fixed shape of policy in London, and no matter how it was twisted or turned, the result would be an end to the cherished rights of Americans. Mason saw no other meaning in the British acts.

Action became the watchword along the Potomac. Early in June, 1774, Mason was urged by Washington to accept a seat in the House of Burgesses. Resisting this entreaty he joined with other Fairfax County gentry to raise a subscription of £273 in hard-to-come-by cash, thirty-eight barrels of flour, and one hundred and fifty bushels of wheat for the locked-in citizens of Boston. After preliminary conferences among the county justices a general meeting of the Fairfax County freeholders was called on July 18 at Alexandria. There Chairman Washington ordered read to the assembly twenty-four resolutions Mason had drafted. The squire of Gunston Hall had been busy since his return.

Washington hardly needed to ask the freeholders whether they subscribed to the propositions that so completely reflected the Whig position. Known as the Fairfax Resolves, these resolutions spelled out the situation for patriots in every crossroad of the colonies. First, the colonies were British, and freeholders (that is, white males who met the property requirement for voting) were entitled to the rights of Englishmen. Second, if constitutional rights were denied them, colonists were justified in resorting to extralegal devices. To accomplish these ends, colonial unity was urged by means of a renewed boycott on English goods (with the hope that "an entire stop" could be put to the "wicked, cruel, and unnatural" slave trade) and the calling of a Continental Congress to meet and act on common problems.

A conciliatory tone was evident in the resolves, but Mason's idea plainly was that any return to the "good old days" before 1763 would come only with colonies standing erect, not returning to grace with bended knees. Similar resolutions that featured a boycott of British goods were adopted elsewhere. A convention called at Williamsburg in August sent a distinguished delegation to the Continental Congress. Only by adamant refusal to serve did Mason himself avoid election to the House of Burgesses. The emergency committee to enforce the Fairfax Resolves became the county committee of safety, with Mason serving on this body to watch the imports of merchants for contraband, publicize the names of violators, and generally promote the patriot cause. Mason also oversaw the enrollment of the Fairfax Independent Company of militiamen, putting it on a businesslike basis with the explanation that its formation for colonial defense "will obviate the pretence of a necessity for taxing us on that account."

In short, the colonists would take care of themselves, whether it involved raising taxes to buy a musket or will power to use it.

About the same time that Mason stood for a fitting of his Fairfax Company uniform, with its blue coat, buff piping, "sling cartouch box and tomahawk," the news from England further quashed his hopes for western land gains. The Quebec Act, extending boundaries of the Canadian province to the banks of the Ohio, came as a severe setback to dreams of huge northwestern tracts of land. All of the time and money Mason had poured into the venture seemed a dead loss, against which his research in land laws and charters—study that had made him an expert on Virginia legal history—dwindled in value to a simple intellectual exercise.

Indeed every bit of news from England seemed to indicate that the grand old fabric of the British constitution was in tatters. The King ignored the petitions from the Continental Congress; the ministry pursued a course that Mason regarded as proof of more punitive and vindictive measures in store. Hence he busied himself with trying to collect the levies for arming the militia, worried with the drafting of a bill for navigation of the Potomac, and tried to speed up shipment of his tobacco under the non-exportation deadline.

Mason's better judgment seemed to indicate that the atmosphere of crisis would lead to some break. Perhaps he believed the showdown might come in Virginia. That it came at Lexington and Concord was no particular surprise. He had long predicted that coercion would bring ruin, perhaps to all parties.

The pall of smoke over Lexington green meant that arms would decide the issue, but Mason thought there was to be more to the struggle than military conquests. His philosophy of what the war with England would have to mean was spelled out when he addressed the Fairfax Company on behalf of his plan to elect militia officers annually. There he broached ideas that were fundamental to his political thought:

> All men are by nature born equally free and independent . . . Every society, all government, and every kind of civil

compact therefore, is or ought to be, calculated for the
general good and safety of the community . . . in all our
agreements let us never lose sight of this fundamental
maxim—that all power was originally lodged in, and consequently is derived from, the people. . . .

These expressions, gleaned from Locke, Sidney, and other English political theorists who were the models for his generation,
focused attention ever more closely on Mason. Washington had
been called to Cambridge to command the infant colonial army
and a vacancy existed in the county delegation to the legislature.
Could a man who insisted that the will of the people should be
supreme, who believed that such a maxim ought to be "buckled
on as our armour," be allowed to stand on the sidelines of the
great struggle that was shaping up?

The Fairfax County freeholders did not think so. To fill
Washington's vacant post in the forthcoming Richmond Convention, the county voters turned to Mason. To avoid service Mason
gave reasons of business and health, adding his "duty to a poor
little helpless family of orphans to whom I now must act the part
of father and mother both." Doubtless a firm neighbor used the
argument, certainly a formidable one after Bunker Hill, that with
able-bodied men serving on the battle lines, other men of ability
left behind had heavy obligations to their country. Whatever the
arguments may have been, Mason gave in to them. The consistent
course frankly required him to stand beside and not behind the
leaders of the patriot group. However reluctantly, Mason accepted
his credentials as a delegate. The language he had used in writing
his will two years earlier could explain this about-face, for he had
then urged his sons to shun public service unless "the necessity of
the times" called them forth "to transmit to their posterity those
sacred rights to which [they] themselves were born."

The spring of 1775 was such a time. Mason depended on James, his able servant, to arrange the details of packing. While the horses pranced impatiently he took his farewell with a sad brood of youngsters, probably gave out more parental advice than he needed to, and reluctantly climbed into the carriage. The whip cracked, the carriage lurched, and George Mason was on his way to Richmond.

CHAPTER FOUR

Crisis at Williamsburg

As he rode south, Mason reflected on his two sorrowful years as a widower, and on the ominous prospect facing the Colony. The same month Ann died, March, 1773, the House of Burgesses in Williamsburg set up a "Committee of Correspondence and Inquiry" to keep in close touch with events in Virginia's sister colonies. A course of unified action thereby took form; and well it did, for when irate Bostonians drowned 342 chests of taxable tea in their harbor Lord North swiftly retaliated. Continued repression from London increased, inevitably, the temper of resistance in the colonies. In the spring of 1774 the First Continental Congress voted drastic economic sanctions against Great Britain. But before they were to take effect, a year later, conflict removed the necessity for them.

In March of 1775, Patrick Henry, in a Richmond speech that made "liberty or death" the most renowned alternative of the

Revolution, asked "that this colony be immediately put into a posture of defence." A month later, Governor Dunmore removed the gunpowder from the Magazine in Williamsburg. In a hastily issued broadside the *Virginia Gazette* summed up the critical state of relations with England: "It is now full time for us all to be on our guard, and to prepare ourselves against every contingency. The sword is now drawn, and God knows when it will be sheathed." There was little debating of that point. Dunmore had fled, and Virginia was without a government when Mason arrived in Richmond in July.

In the heat of a Tidewater summer there was little to choose between Richmond and Williamsburg. Yet while Dunmore kept alive the possibility that he might return at the head of an invasion force and seize Williamsburg, it seemed prudent to the Virginians to meet inland. Each day's session reminded Mason by contrast of the pleasant life at Gunston Hall. As often as he could he wrote to his childless neighbor, Martin Cockburn, who was keeping an affectionate eye on the Mason children. "This is hard duty," he told Cockburn. The committee charged with the complex task of raising and paying for an army met after breakfast each morning and worked until the regular session of the Convention began. After adjournment at five o'clock Mason barely had time for dinner "and a little refreshment" before the group resumed its labors by candlelight. It was the kind of tedious committee work he had hoped to avoid.

His stature as a delegate precluded that. Sick or healthy, Mason was needed for his ability. During lulls in a session he could go out to the local apothecaries to replenish his supply of ginseng and calomel. But seldom was he inclined to complicate his duties by more travel than that. "Though I was exceedingly indisposed for several days," he wrote to Cockburn, "kind and hospitable treatment from a neighboring country gentleman has recovered me."

When a vacancy in the Virginia delegation to the Continental Congress had to be filled, his colleagues insisted that he accept the appointment. Embarrassed by the likely chance of being ordered to Philadelphia, Mason rose "to make a public excuse, & give my reasons for refusal; in doing which I felt myself more distress'd than ever I was in my life, especially when I saw tears run down the President's cheeks."

The misty eyes of Peyton Randolph left Mason touched but unyielding. He escaped a trip beyond the Potomac, but the effect of his refusal moved him to accept a seat on the powerful, busy Committee of Safety that served in lieu of an established government. Still mildly protesting the assignment, Mason privately regarded it as "even more inconvenient and disagreeable to me than going to the Congress." When later he tried to resign the appointment, the delegates "answered by an universal no."

Fortunately the pace of Convention business quickened during the next few days, and the prospect of concluding it promised a measure of relief. Before the final session Mason was sought out by a group of British-born merchants who were suspected of being Tories. Sympathetically, he drafted a general test oath for the frightened tradesmen which they readily signed. With that act he took leave of legislative duties, headed for Fairfax County and home.

Resting again at Gunston Hall, Mason regarded his recent Richmond venture as a sound argument for retirement from political affairs. He wrote General Washington at Cambridge that the Convention had been torn with factions. The pettifogging had disgusted Mason to the point of despair. Could such men defy the power of Great Britain, when they snarled at each other over picayune matters? "Mere vexation and disgust threw me into such an ill state of health, that before the Convention rose," he lamented, "I was sometimes near fainting in the House." Not until the "babblers" had been silenced was any real progress made. Immodestly, Mason gave credit for the accomplishments of the session to "a few weighty members."

During the fall and winter this need for heavy-thinking members to hold down the light-headed "babblers" may have prompted Mason's decision to return to the Convention of 1776. The factionalism exhibited at Richmond showed itself at the polls, with a marked spirit of dissent abroad that ended the cut-and-dried pattern of earlier contests. Other events indicated that Virginians had cause for mounting uneasiness. The ousted Governor Dunmore had terrorized the lower coast, and rumors had him appearing at every convenient landing point with torch in hand. Mason took the precaution of temporarily moving his family away from Gunston Hall and advised General Washington's lady to follow his example. The whereabouts of the main British army that in a midnight evacuation had left Boston was still a mystery. Was it bound for Nova Scotia, New York, or perhaps some southern port near Williamsburg?

Upset by the endless rumors and by the seeming lack of action, stirred by Tom Paine's *Common Sense* that had swept through the colonies in midwinter, the freeholders almost removed Mason into his coveted retirement. Voluntary retirement was a constant threat he liked to make. But a forced retreat from the Convention that loomed as the most important assemblage in the Colony's history was something else. Spared that humiliation by a narrow margin of victory, Mason readied his affairs for the May trip to Williamsburg. It would be dusty and hot on the road, and the inns would be a poor substitute for the comfort of Gunston Hall. Yet if Washington's men could dodge musket balls in the cause of liberty Mason was ready to fight bedbugs in a wayside tavern.

A rival candidate Mason could defeat, but he was no match for the gout. When the May session was scheduled to begin, he was bedridden with a "smart fit" of it that forced him to postpone his departure. Meanwhile the last vestige of imperial government died a quiet death as the delegates began to arrive in Williamsburg. Meeting on May 6, only a few of the old burgesses bothered to attend the last session of the House, leaving the clerk to write "FINIS" in their journal with a flamboyant brush of his quill.

The royal regime *was* finished, for the last thoughts of reconciliation had perished during the winter when the British Navy openly bombarded coastal towns, when foreign mercenaries arrived to fight for George III, and when the newspapers everywhere rang with calls for independence. Public opinion, in fact, seemed to be outpacing public leadership. A Williamsburg observer sensed the situation and warned Richard Henry Lee that independence must be declared or "we are all ruined." As the delegates assembled in the capital, General Charles Lee sized them up confidently: "There is a noble spirit in this Province, pervading all orders of men; if the same becomes universal, we shall be saved."

The chances for political salvation in Virginia rested in able hands. While Washington, Jefferson, and other distinguished Virginians served beyond the borders of the Colony, a number of capable men had been chosen for Convention service. Patrick Henry, master of persuasive eloquence, was on hand. Representatives from the older eastern counties included Edmund Pendleton, Thomas Ludwell Lee, Archibald Cary, and the still-absent Mason. The western counties sent a smaller band, leaving to the Tidewater group its traditional leadership.

Pendleton was selected president, thus placing the gavel in the hands of a renowned lawyer of moderate tendencies. Like Mason, Pendleton had reluctantly seen his concept of the British Constitution slowly dissolve after 1765. Any doubts the two men might have harbored, or any caution that conservatives might have urged at this juncture, would have been lost in the clamor being set up by their outspoken constituents. Typical of the popular expressions was the petition from Buckingham County, where the voting freeholders urged the Convention immediately to declare Virginia free and establish "a free and happy Constitution."

In that vein petition followed petition as it became obvious that the time for argument had passed. There was no atmosphere for debate, and Henry's oratory was a surplus weapon in a lopsided contest. Sentiment for total separation from the Empire focused ultimately on a resolution instructing the Virginia delegates at Philadelphia to urge the Continental Congress to declare the colonies free. On May 15 the resolution passed with no voice raised in dissent. For the consequences of such a bold step, some preparations had already been made in Richmond. But they were far from complete.

While local citizens celebrated the resolution with a military display "of great exactness," Mason was still en route to Williamsburg. Arrived, he found that a more matter-of-fact resolution had also been passed calling for the drafting of a declaration of rights and a "plan of government"—a business of such obvious magnitude that a huge committee had been appointed for the task. Mason was promptly added. The group would have found its work hampered by the sheer number of its members had not a firm hand taken charge. Archibald Cary was the chairman, but it was Mason who dominated the committee.

The job of drafting concrete proposals for the new government fell to Mason for several reasons. In the first place he was qualified by background. No man knew more about colonial charters or what the law books said about rights and proper constitutions. The lawyers present acknowledged that. More important from Mason's viewpoint was the need to get on with the project at once, without a lot of useless wasting of time over proposals and procedures. To a close friend he confided that the committee was "according to custom overcharged with useless members." Where some historians have looked back on the Convention as an illustrious body of men, Mason dismissed many of his colleagues' abilities with a wave of the hand. The defects of the last assembly, he declared, had not been mended by the recent elections. Instead of getting down to fundamental propositions the committee, he glumly predicted, would offer "a thousand ridiculous and impracticable proposals," all of them unacceptable to men of good sense. How could this disastrous prospect be avoided? "Only by a few men of integrity and abilities, whose country's interest lies next to their hearts, undertaking this business and defending it ably through every stage of opposition."

Whatever else he might have been, Mason was not patient. The traditional routine of parliamentary procedure bored him. He detested committee work. A forceful personality, he pitched headlong into the business that demanded priority: a statement of those rights held by all people, individually and in association with each other. His work table was littered with notes, with foolscap, with law books. They were his raw material, and he likely supplemented them now and then from the libraries of George Wythe or the College of William and Mary.

Behind committee doors Mason suppressed his petulance, knowing that speed was important. There was no tortuous arguing out of every detailed item, every choice of verb or noun. That would have given him more anguish than a siege of gout. A few of the collaborators, notably Thomas Ludwell Lee, helped to guide the composition of the document, though the dispatch with which it appeared carried no hint of the lifetime of thought applied to the problems involved. The insistent language of county petitions also had its accelerating effect: demands for full representation, for free and frequent elections; dark hints about the danger of standing armies. These expressions of wide discontent were joined under Mason's hand to the historic experience of men versus governments. Young Edmund Randolph, awed by the blend of ability and technique he saw in Mason's work, later recalled that the committee had received many suggestions for a bill of rights and a constitution but that they revealed more ambition than political sagacity. The plan "proposed by George Mason swallowed up all the rest, by fixing the grounds" for the final draft.

The muggy Williamsburg climate in the late spring of 1776 was heavy with more than humidity. Questions of purpose and direction called for immediate attention; practical problems of interim government demanded the authority of a constitution, for the commonwealth was drifting without a legal rudder. Pendleton reported to Jefferson at Philadelphia that the delegates feared a long session but would "sweat it out with fortitude." "The political cooks are busy in preparing the dish, and as Colo. Mason seems to have the ascendancy in the great work, I have sanguine hopes it will be framed so as to answer it's end," the president wrote. That end, of course, was "prosperity to the community and security to individuals."

A few days later the guessing game ended. Mason stood aside and Archibald Cary presented the Convention with a draft of the Virginia Declaration of Rights. To ten basic articles prepared by Mason the drafting committee appears to have added four more. Cary, whose hard-bitten qualities had earned him the nickname of "Old Iron," stood up and read the proposals to the delegates. Most of them liked what they heard. Here and there among the benches where the members sat a few mumbled misgivings were audible. Someone called for a vote to print and distribute copies to the delegates, and before the required third reading of the document there seemed every possibility that Mason might have to defend the proposals before his old adversaries, the prattling politicians.

After each delegate studied the proposals, the general debate opened on a sour note. Thomas Ludwell Lee lamented in his

THOMAS JEFFERSON, *one of the intellectual spokesmen of the American Revolution. Like Mason, a scholar, he differed from him in his lively taste for public life.*

nightly letter-writing sessions that "a certain set of aristocrats" had thrown up a line of defense in an effort to keep control of the Convention in conservative hands. Led by Robert Carter Nicholas, the old guard "kept us at bay on the first line" of the draft, Lee reported. Nicholas challenged the statement that all men are created equally free and independent. In a slaveholding society, the argument ran, all men were obviously not born free and equal. To pretend otherwise, the conservatives suggested, was to invite civil war on their own estates.

For Mason this opening argument from the opposition struck a tender nerve. In all likelihood, he had really intended to establish a claim that Americans were free and equal with Englishmen. However, he had long wrestled with the slave problem and in earlier writings had gone out of his way to make not-very-subtle remarks about it. As early as 1765 he had questioned the practice of slavery both for its economic principle and for its effect on the "morals and manners of our people." Other gentry had occasionally sympathized with this attitude though with no display of enthusiasm. Now the argument shifted to a new ground. Slaves held no property. Indeed, slaves were property, and hence they were not "constituent members of our society" and "could never pretend to any benefit from such a maxim."

By raising the slavery issue, almost before the delegates were settled in their seats, the conservatives went straight to the heart of the problem facing the Convention. How far was the course of freedom to run? Carter Braxton, in modern terms a reactionary, had one answer: merely take the British Constitution back to its original state and remedy its imperfections. The practical suggestions he offered for doing that promised to create more imperfections than they remedied. One of Mason's closest friends denounced the pamphlet Braxton wrote as a "contemptible little tract." And contemptible it was to the ardent revolutionists, but

it still represented a point of view to be reckoned with. To con-
demn was not enough.

Mason, furthermore, was still at work on a constitution that
would follow upon the Declaration of Rights and embody in concrete form many of its recommendations, such as three separate
branches of government and annual elections for representatives,
who would have the purse strings in their hands. The conservatives sensed the nature of the radical program and maneuvered
for a position that would enable them to hold the more vociferous
patriots in check. For four days they wrangled over the question
of equality, blocking debate on the rest of the declaration.

Mason waited, fretful, annoyed.

His aide on the drafting committee, Thomas Ludwell Lee,
thought that this stumbling on the threshold of the whole business might wreck the Convention. If every step were to be equally
difficult, no one could predict when the haggling would end. Lee
eyed the conservatives as "monsters," but like the rest at last
assented to a device that cut through the discord.

As finally approved, the first sentence read "That all men are
by nature equally free and independent, and have certain inherent
rights, of which, *when they enter into a state of society,* they cannot, by any compact, deprive or divest their posterity; . . ." The
italicized phrase, with its implicit proposition that slaves are not
members of society, placated the opposition.

There is no record of Mason's reaction to the concession. It is
likely that he yielded the point only out of political necessity and
because of a suspicion that a stiffer fight for it would make the
delegates even more argumentative on equally farsighted articles
still to be debated.

If so, he was right. Sparse entries in the Convention journal
tell little of what took place on the floor. During the five days of
general discussion, Mason employed oratory "neither flowing nor
smooth, but his language was strong, his manner most impressive,

(Copy of the first Draught by G M.)

A Declaration of Rights made by the
Representatives of the good People of Virginia,
assembled in full and free Convention; which
Rights do pertain to them and their Posterity,
as the Basis and Foundation of Government.

1. That all Men are created equally free & independent, & have
certain inherent natural Rights, of which they can not by
any Compact deprive or divest their Posterity; among which
are the Enjoyment of Life & Liberty, with the Means of acquiring &
possessing Property, & pursuing & obtaining Happiness & Safety.

2. That all Power is by God & Nature vested in, & consequently
derived from the People; that Magistrates are their Trustees &
Servants, and at all Times amenable to them.

3. That Government is or ought to be instituted for the
common Benefit, Protection & Security of the People, Nation
or Community. Of all the various Modes & Forms of Government that is best which is capable of producing the greatest
Degree of Happiness & Safety, & is most effectually secured against
the Danger of mal-administration, and that whenever any Government shall be found inadequate or contrary to these purposes, a Majority of the Community hath an indubitable, unalienable & indefeasible Right to reform, alter, or abolish it, in
such

THE FIRST PAGE of a draft of the Virginia Declaration of Rights in
Mason's hand. At the end of the draft, Mason took note of the few
alterations it received, "some of them not for the better."

and strengthened by a dash of biting cynicism when provocation made it seasonable." If he winced when the delegates inked over several of his rhetorical flourishes, he did not sulk. Nor was he affronted when his references to God and nature were transposed into the more practical language of common law, of eighteenth-century legal practice in the colony of Virginia.

In the final hours of debate several articles inserted by the drafting committee (on ex post facto laws and bills of attainder) were voted down, mainly because Patrick Henry warned that "some towering public offender" might find them a cloak for his wrong-doing. It is clear when we piece the surviving information together that Mason had captured the spirit of the Convention. Nothing he considered vital was rejected. To his basic framework of ten provisions six more finally were added as a result of committee action and debate. He thought the additions rather out of place, but in public debate compromises had to be made. The people expected action, not endless discussion.

Dismayed by the superficial abilities of some delegates, Mason impatiently awaited the final vote. It had been a busy fortnight, with each trip back to his lodgings ending a weary day of accomplishment. By candlelight he could write to friends of his suffering and endurance, but in fact the business proceeded with rare speed. In less than four weeks from the appointment of the committee, the job was over. The final draft of the Declaration of Rights had its required third reading and passed the Convention unanimously on June 12.

The intellectual armament Mason brought to the debates had been in perfect working order. Unconsciously he had been preparing for just such an encounter since he first stepped into his uncle's library at Marlborough. Mason knew the strengths and weaknesses of the ancient republics as well as he knew the strengths and weaknesses of his Gunston Hall field hands. He had charted his way so thoroughly through English constitutional history that

every significant precedent was recorded in his mind as a guide-
post for future reference. He had become convinced, as hours and
days had melted into months of study, that there was a mystical
kind of *natural* law at work in this world that, if made a matter
of practice, would surely put an end to the bondage of ignorance.

The British Constitution had been the best effort so far toward achieving this. A better instrument could be formed. Of
that he was as certain as he was that the time had come to form
it. So were Thomas Jefferson and the others in Mason's circle who
were bothered by the "what is" and "what ought to be" of human
affairs. It was no accident that most of Mason's provisions contained "ought." It was the key word in his effort to square actual
practices with his vision of the ideal guide to government.

The Declaration of Rights, as he fashioned it, was buttressed
by the writings of all those Englishmen who had ever struggled
with courts and kings over constitutional questions. John Locke
and Algernon Sidney, long since in their graves, were alive once
again in his sentences. Infected by their spirit of English liberal-
ism, Mason simply added to abstracts of their writings the specific
causes of American concern. He wrote as an English-American,
working on behalf of rights that arose from natural law and were
assumed to be the birthrights of every free American. Those rights
were also anchored deep in English common law and in the history of the American colonies. Certain men in high places now
had questioned whether the colonies had become, like delinquent
children, too obstreperous to be trusted with them.

Mason's declaration opened with a strong statement: all men
are by nature free and have certain basic rights that cannot be
tampered with, "the enjoyment of life and liberty, with the means
of acquiring and possessing property, and pursuing and obtaining
happiness and safety." Here, said Mason, was the true end of good
government. (The dark contradiction of slavery did not conform
to this bright new world he was conceiving, and it already worried

him deeply as a nightmare in the making.) And that men are entitled to the means of *acquiring* and possessing property marked an historic advance from John Locke's trilogy of rights—life, liberty, and property—that simply endorsed *ownership* of property.

The statements that followed were cast in straightforward language. Simply arranged in a few hundred words, they were ideas that announced man's native freedom from restraint unless he threatened or did harm to others. The few rules needed to keep affairs orderly could be worked out by representatives elected annually. The delegates so chosen would reflect absolutely the will and wisdom of their constituents.

A good deal of dressing went onto this simple framework, of course, but the phrasing did not obscure the basic ideas. Leave men alone and they will be clever enough to see that freedom and tolerance best serve their self-interests and permit them to enjoy the blessings of life and property. That is true liberty and the unfettered pursuit of happiness.

As a natural corollary, the government erected must be severely held within limits even though it is a creation of the popular will. Mason and his generation distrusted government ("administration" was their word for it) whether it was of their own making or decreed from across the Atlantic. The vilest curse that could befall a people was a government disposed to do evil; hence the people at all times had the right to "reform, alter, or abolish it, in such manner as shall be judged most conducive to the public weal." Thus Mason stated the rights of man in one of the boldest and most liberal expressions ever set down on paper. Contained within it was an unlimited faith in free men to make the proper decision under any circumstances. A government is the creation of the people, who can maintain or abolish it—whichever they choose. This was not philosophical speculation, an hypothesis for quiet, fireside analysis. It was a course of action.

If we credit Mason for the felicitious outpouring of his ideas, his colleagues also deserve recognition. Surely Mason was putting into articulate form the ideas held by most of the Virginia patriots. The cogency, clarity, and brevity of them we owe to Mason's good judgment, but if he had not chosen wisely his words and ideas the Declaration of Rights might never have survived the Convention debate. The articles dealing with annual elections, the separation of the government into three branches, the arbitrary suspension of laws, criminal court procedure, and the ban on standing armies all sprang from both an English heritage and an American vexation with misused power. Colonial householders had seen their doors forced open by Crown agents who arrested and ransacked without legal authority. High-handed army officers had contemptuously flouted civil authority. Some of these grievances Virginians had personally experienced, while through their public prints and private letters they knew of others. Recent happenings in the colonies completed disillusionment with the mother country. If the gamble of revolution paid off the future would allow no meddling with a man's rights.

Had the Virginia declaration pointed out no new directions in terms of individual freedom, it would still deserve acclaim for its articulate recital of fundamental liberties.

But Mason and the Convention went further. "That the freedom of the press is one of the great bulwarks of liberty, and can never be restrained but by despotick governments," read Article XII. Men had been talking about a free press for generations, on both sides of the Atlantic, but since 1690 Americans had seen printers harassed by authorities acting under the common law concept of sedition. The Zenger case had done nothing to settle the question of how far newspapers might go in their criticism of public officials. The Stamp Act crisis, in a sense, had. The press had then taken the bull by the horns. By 1776 the proposition was clearly established, the sentiment so favorable that there was no need later to strengthen Article XII by more specific statutes.

The local printer could henceforth fill up his galleys without one eye on the sheriff's office. The local dissenter from the established Church stood ultimately to gain comparable license; the first step toward it lay in the article on religion. It was one of the most prophetic and farsighted provisions of the Virginia Declaration of Rights:

> That religion, or the duty which we owe to our Creator, and the manner of discharging it, can be directed only by reason and conviction, not by force or violence, and therefore, all men are equally entitled to the free exercise of religion, according to the dictates of conscience; and that it is the mutual duty of all to practise Christian forbearance, love, and charity, towards each other.

The wording seems to have been Mason's, except for the "free exercise" that young James Madison, then on the threshold of his career, suggested to broaden the original word "toleration." It was a decisive change. By it religious *freedom* became a right; religious *toleration* would have been merely a concession. Every delegate of course knew about the Baptist preachers who were fined and jailed for holding services without permission from the General Court in Williamsburg. Was it proper, in an enlightened age, to fine a man or lock him up for haranguing a crowd on the virtue of full immersion as a way of saving souls? Presbyterians and Methodists usually asked for Court permission, but they likewise were taxed to support the Anglican Church they refused to be a part of.

Yet it was a vestryman of the Anglican Church, abetted by the youthful but brilliant Madison, who proposed to change all that.

Mason and the other delegates sensed the liberal spirit of the times, aware that most Virginians were revolted by the useless persecutions they had witnessed. A decade earlier Mason had compared the British crackdown on Americans to "persecution in matters of religion . . . (which) serves not to extinguish but to confirm the heresy." A pillar in Truro Parish, he nevertheless believed that each man was responsible to "Divine Providence" in his own way. Following through with the idea, his associates, Madison and Jefferson, carried the matter to a conclusion ten years later in the Virginia Statute for Religious Freedom that removed the last traces of a state-supported church in Virginia.

On May 15, 1776, the resolution proposing independence had been noisily dispatched by parades and artillery salutes. If the Declaration of Rights was celebrated at all it was to the accompaniment of nothing more ceremonial than uplifted tankards in stuffy tap rooms along lower Duke of Gloucester Street. But then such toasts could easily have been mistaken for the practical solution to a recurrent problem; the humid Tidewater summer already had returned for its annual four months' visit.

More work lay ahead.

For the year Virginia had operated with only a provisional, "homemade" government, the momentum of the old colonial system had been strong enough to keep the Colony out of internal trouble. Now, with war adding new tests to the problem of governing, a written constitution was as imperative as gunpowder and lead. The Declaration of Rights was a statement of principles, a credo, an affirmation of the respect that should exist between people and government. It was, having been created, a mighty symbol of Mason's "take nothing for granted" caution, of the passion for detail that led him to insist so often upon a "frequent recurrence to fundamental principles." But the Declaration, without a constitution, was a conscience in search of a mind, a kind of motionless morality awaiting directions. The draft of a constitution that soon appeared on the floor of the Convention contained directions, chiefly from the mind of George Mason.

The arrival of Mason's draft was not followed by the show of hostility from conservatives who at first had been so contentious about the Declaration of Rights. However, the constitution became no less an object for hammering and reshaping on the anvil of debate, even though the forging took less time. On June 29, almost a week before the Declaration of Independence was declared in Philadelphia, the Virginia Constitution was a fact.

" 'Tis very much of the democratic kind," said one of the members. Delegates were to be chosen annually by the people for a lower house, senators elected to an upper house for four-year terms. The governor assumed office for one year on election by the two houses, who also appointed eight men to a council of state to "advise" the governor. All laws were to initiate in the House of Delegates. The judicial duties, formerly a prerogative of the Governor's Council, were transferred to a new system of courts.

To Richard Henry Lee, who had made the remark, it was more democratic than anything in his previous experience. And he probably used the word "democratic" because the House of Delegates was now completely in charge of the government. But the suffrage requirements* were unchanged, and there was little pretense at an equal distribution of powers among executive, legislative, and judicial branches. The governor himself became little more than a figurehead, powerless to veto legislation or to suggest amendments without the approval of his council of state. Such a constitution measured the force of colonial reaction against a strong executive.

It also assured that with independence won a flurry of second thoughts would challenge much of the constitution. Subsequent

----

* Ownership of a house and lot in town, or twenty-five acres with "a house and plantation" on it, or one hundred undeveloped acres.

calls for revision would dwell heavily on the point that the people themselves had been given no chance to ratify it. Apart from that, many of the statements in the Declaration of Rights had still to be translated into facts by a constitution. The time was not politically ripe for activating every ideal. Yet Mason can hardly be reproached for lacking a wholehearted sense of public trust that was still fifty years away. The faith implied by the new era that ushered in Jacksonian democracy was but an extension of the faith that underlay Mason's approach to self-rule in 1776.

The Convention of 1776 adjourned. Delegates who had entered the Capitol as British subjects took their leave of Williamsburg as citizens of a new commonwealth. A final round of Madeira, some nervous congratulations, and it was all over. The work had gone well, considering the size of the job that had to be done.

Mason the legislator had completed his assignment, but Mason the father had one further duty. Supplies of ribbons, buckles, buttons, and other elemental fineries from abroad were drying up. Young Masons at home would expect a few such presents from the shops along Duke of Gloucester Street. Those purchases packed away in his traveling trunk, he settled down in the carriage—his brown hair now streaked with gray, his face fuller and his frame stouter than when he had arrived in Williamsburg as a burgess seventeen years earlier. As the carriage rolled northward toward Port Royal, Fredericksburg, and home, Mason pondered the business that had been finished: the design and construction of a new government. At Gunston Hall he would have plenty of time to ponder the still harder task—making it work.

CHAPTER FIVE

Victory—and New Conflict

IN December of 1770 Mason declared that Americans regarded independence as "the wildest chimera that ever disturbed a madman's brain." Like sensitive adolescents, the colonies bridled at the rebukes of their elders, without being quite ready to run away from home. Scarcely half a decade later the bonds of family loyalty, scorched and weakened by the heat of dispute and dissension, parted. Loyalty turned into treason, rebellion became patriotism. Those who clung to the old allegiance either said nothing about it, or privately made plans to close out their affairs. The public cancellation of the old loyalty on July 4, 1776, was something less than a "wild chimera" created by the lunatic fringe. The idea of independence had grown by neatly rational stages into a popular revolution. The ancient poets, Mason now reflected, "made a kind of being out of necessity, and tell us that the gods

themselves are obliged to yield to her." Yielding before this determined necessity was the comfortable pragmatism that for years had
guided England's colonial policy.

It was to be a gentleman's revolt, prefaced by no tawdry palace
conspiracy, no rush to man the barricades. An elaborate under-
ground network of inspired patriots would have been dramatic
but superfluous. Committees of Correspondence operated openly.
Likewise, manifestoes and declarations could be distributed and
discussed as openly as the latest shipping news. There was no need
to slip them furtively from hand to hand.

The Virginia Convention of 1776 was an assembly dominated
by silk-stocking rebels. Before it adjourned, the rousing language
of Mason's draft of the Declaration of Rights was being read up
and down the Atlantic seaboard. When the Declaration finally
passed on June 12, Philadelphia newspapers had already printed
the provisions in several editions. Copies of the *Evening Post* and
Gazette spread northward in the saddlebags of post riders or in
the pouches of accommodating sea captains. The *Virginia Gazette,*
in similar fashion, sent the news to the Carolinas and Georgia.

Publication of the draft could not have been more timely. Out
from the Continental Congress had gone an urgent injunction to
all the colonies to set up their own governments in a *de facto* act
of independence. John Adams, indulging in shrewd Yankee flattery, stated that all eyes were on the Virginians, that the other
colonies would look to them for leadership. Fact as well as flattery
rode on the remark. In no colony was there any scarcity of advice,
but it was as though they all were waiting for someone to signal
the awesome finality of independence. The meeting in Williamsburg replaced advice with action. John's cousin Samuel, finding
the Virginia Declaration in his mail, informed the sender that it
would be "a feast to our little circle." To be sure, it was. Samuel's
little circle was the group of delegates meeting in Philadelphia.

The early appearance of the Virginia draft was heartening and positive support to the convention assembled there. Mason's Declaration brought a message of hope for a better, more politically stabilized life bound securely to the proposition that man's dignity is his most sacred possession. In his statement were the aspirations of the coming revolution, the ideals essential to the endurance of individual dignity and liberty under law that was not subject to arbitrary whims of a ruler. The Philadelphia group, with Jefferson as its draftsman, proclaimed the details of colonial anger in a more sweeping, more bitterly indicting document. But its purpose was to condition Americans to the end of the old regime and to justify, in the brash language of propaganda, the break with England.

The Declaration of Independence was an irrevocable pledge to action. By it the colonies were all committed. Beginning to fight a war—the next step—was automatic. It could not wait until individual state governments were set up within the embryonic confederation of states. Nevertheless the latter business got under way promptly.

Pennsylvania shook off the old royal vestments in a matter of weeks and prefaced its constitution with a declaration of rights "taken almost verbatim" from the Virginia draft. Fourteen of its sixteen articles bore the stamp of the Williamsburg assembly. In Maryland the constitutional committee borrowed wholesale from the Mason model, adding bans on ex post facto laws and bills of attainder to a firm specification that prohibited future legislative tampering with the bill of rights "on any pretence whatever." Delaware patriots gave their endorsement to Mason's statements and appended a section forbidding the importation of slaves, a provision Mason would have championed more vigorously in Virginia had such a course not been, on the face of it, politically foolhardy. North Carolina's bill of rights seemed to stray far afield in offering a protective guarantee for the hunting grounds of certain

Indian tribes, but inclusion of the article reflected the healthy zeal with which men everywhere were attempting to translate the "natural rights of men" into a practical set of rules.

North Carolina was the fifth state to adopt a declaration of rights before the fateful year 1776 dropped from the calendar. If the year had been short on military victories it had been long on ideological triumphs. And by the time the last cannonade of the Revolution sounded every state either had fashioned a separate bill of rights or had passed statutes with similar provisions.* In a good many cases the work was done with scissors, pastepot, and a copy of the Virginia Declaration—a fact that did not escape Mason's notice. Some time later when he sent a copy to a cousin in England he observed that it had been "closely imitated by all the other states."

But for now, Mason was too busy to collect accolades for his achievement. During the late summer of 1776 he spent much of his time, in that spirit of fresh dedication that always marks the beginning of war, helping to arrange defenses for Fairfax County. Habitually tardy at legislative sessions, he showed up at Williamsburg in mid-November and explained away his absence on "good cause" to avoid the fine levied by the House of Delegates. Delegate Mason soon found that only the name of the lower chamber was altered; his duties were as numerous as ever, and he was as busy a delegate as he had ever been a burgess.

Much of the work was of his own making, for the House was soon wrangling over the knotty religious issue that had not been settled by the mere provision for freedom of conscience stated in the Declaration of Rights. Having declared in June that all men

---

* In New York, New Jersey, Georgia, and South Carolina personal rights were provided for in constitutions and statutes, not in separate documents. Connecticut and Rhode Island continued to operate under their colonial charters.

are equally entitled to the free exercise of religion, the Virginia lawmakers were faced in November by the embarrassing truism that "all promises have predicates." Dissenting congregations, specifically Baptists and Presbyterians, looked upon the grand words as promise of the same recognition enjoyed by Anglicans in the flock of the established Church. The Church, despite the bold statement in the Declaration of Rights, was still maintained by public taxation. With some justice Mason found himself on the committee engulfed by the flood of petitions (one of which contained almost 10,000 names) protesting this discrimination.

Both sides had advocates on the committee. Carter Braxton, he of the reactionary "contemptible little tract," found formidable allies in Edmund Pendleton and Robert Carter Nicholas to range against the liberal Mason and the arch-liberal Jefferson. Sensing that the fight for reforms in Virginia would be a tough one, Jefferson had resigned from the Continental Congress and was back in Williamsburg, temporarily living in the house of his old teacher, George Wythe. Convinced, as Mason was, that the people were outrunning their leaders in the desire for reform, Jefferson insisted on complete religious freedom. Presentation of the dissenters' petitions soon led, as he later recalled, to "the severest contest in which I have ever been engaged."

So torrid grew the debating that finally the entire Assembly took on the job of deciding what had to be done. A compromise bill, drafted by Mason, repudiated the ancient heresy acts of Parliament and freed dissenters from future levies to support the established Church. The rectors came off the public payroll. But the Assembly left itself open for a continual drumfire of protests from every corner of the state because of other prerogatives, notably the right to perform a legally recorded marriage, retained by Anglican clergymen but denied to dissenting ministers. The final severance act was not to come for another decade.

Apart from the hot words generated by the idea of shrinking

the power of an institution in such preferred standing as the Anglican Church, the session was busy but less divided. There were, after all, other things crying for attention. One of them in which Mason's talents predominated was the boundary dispute with Pennsylvania—a curious internal matter in the midst of war, it would seem, but one calling for action in the interest of closer interstate relations. Total success, as in the question of the Church, had to be deferred. More imperative was the matter of extraordinary powers needed by the governor and his council as an emergency war measure. Mason assisted in drawing up that act, then joined in the task of designing a new court system for the state. Another group, lawyers chosen to revise the laws of the commonwealth, included him as the only layman. The last job was so burdensome that he finally bowed out, but not until he had performed yeoman duties in reviewing the criminal and land laws. For a man who could complain with tedious regularity about his poor health, Mason was still quite a workhorse.

But, as he had observed before, if he and few others did not stick around, a few of the "babblers" might erect God-knows-what in place of the old system. Mason was devoted to Virginia, though a taste for crusty hyperbole insured that his affection would never grow sentimental. Williamsburg, however, tested the limits of both his devotion and his fortitude. When he was urged again in 1777 to take one of the Virginia seats in the Continental Congress, Mason excused himself on the plea that a smallpox inoculation had seriously impaired his health.

His old neighbor, George Washington, was eager to learn that Mason's health would at least permit further service in the Virginia Assembly. The harried commander-in-chief had taken note of a rapidly spreading contagion as dangerous as a new shipload of redcoats: inflation. "A rat in the shape of a horse," he lamented, "is not to be bought at this time for less than £200." Would Mason go back to the House of Delegates and take the lead in grappling with this problem of inflation? He would. Meanwhile state printers kept pace with the Continental treasury, issuing paper currency in such quantities that it began to depreciate even before it was lifted from the presses.

As Mason pondered the problem his thoughts turned once again to the millions of acres of Virginia that lay westward beyond the mountains. Could not those lands be the key defense against financial disaster? Logic seemed to say yes. And because it was logical, he proposed that Virginia's western lands be set aside as a sinking fund for the state debts. In this way inflation might be checked by basing the currency obligations on assets more tangible than mere hope. Other states might follow Virginia's example, at least if the tangle of previous grants, many of which conflicted with those of Virginia, could be unraveled. But the likelihood of that was slim; continental solidarity was not yet strong enough to quash that kind of self-interest. Even Mason himself showed no willingness to drop the Ohio Company claim to the 200,000 acres it had already paid to have surveyed. Retention of that, in fact, was a condition of his plan.

Long interest in the west had brought him more than once into contact with the young adventurer George Rogers Clark. The frontiersman now appeared in Williamsburg with a bold plan. He would lead a sweep into the wilderness north of the Ohio River aimed at capturing British outposts. Such an expedition could put a stop to Governor Henry Hamilton's traffic in American scalps and demonstrate American strength (or at least the illusion of it) to sullen Indian tribes and skeptical Spaniards. Another attractive dividend was the possibility that the campaign, paid for by Virginia, would tighten her claim to the entire Northwest Territory.

Mason liked Clark's idea. So did Governor Patrick Henry, Jefferson, and George Wythe. Details of the scheme were perfected in private. The four men committed themselves to work

THE CAPITOL IN WILLIAMSBURG. *In spite of the greater distance between Gunston Hall and Williamsburg, Mason unsuccessfully opposed the transfer of the capital to Richmond.*

out a land bounty award for Clark's volunteers and handed him a letter authorizing the enterprise. All could be lost, they reasoned, if the secrecy of Clark's intention became public knowledge.

Months passed during which the Assembly returned to Mason's proposal from time to time. Suddenly fate seemed to lend a hand by bringing the electrifying news of Clark's capture of Kaskaskia. Promptly the plan for checking inflation and confirming the land claims acquired new importance. The letdown and final collapse of the plan came less suddenly. An active group within the Virginia Assembly had its own axe to grind in the western country. The best Mason could do was to engineer repudiation of some of the rival claims. His legislative position was not powerful enough to sustain a basically sound idea in the face of vested interests in which he was also a principal.

Preoccupied with Virginia affairs and his own business interests, he in fact became so involved with local concerns that occasionally he lost sight of the Revolution as a united war effort. Deaf to personal pleas from Washington that he serve in the national councils, he on one occasion justified his refusal with the remark that the other Virginia delegates were so lackluster that he could not be blamed "for taking care . . . to keep out of such company." Most of his thoughts were centered on Fairfax County and on Gunston Hall; yet when the Assembly voted to move the capital from Williamsburg to Richmond he was one of the minority who resisted the change despite the shorter, less bothersome carriage ride. But Mason would not budge beyond the borders of Virginia.

Certainly his neighbors, during the lean years of war, appreciated his sincere concern for their interests as well as his own. While insisting that militiamen be kept alert to repel rumored invasions of the Northern Neck, Mason watched one of his own sons march off to the fight, and sat down to write another living in Europe to be on the lookout for a sharp rise in tobacco prices.

Early in 1780, now 54, he remarried. The match with Sarah Brent from nearby Dumfries, some four years younger than Mason, was arranged on business-like terms, as was the custom of the day, giving the second mistress of Gunston Hall only lifetime tenure on the estate if she survived Mason and they had no children. In the unlikely event of more little Masons, the marriage contract provided for Sarah to share fully in the estate. As it turned out no more cribs were set up in the great house during Mason's lifetime. The middle-aged, newly-wedded Mason reluctantly left Fairfax County later in the spring for the new capital at Richmond.

Dusty, unattractive, and swarming with flies, it was a city that held few charms for him, and he found a busy schedule the best antidote for his impatient desire to return home. Mason worked steadily, almost tirelessly, showing an uncanny ability to master details. He hammered away once again for drastic measures that would bolster the sagging state treasury, and he saw the old boundary quarrel with Pennsylvania settled when the Mason and Dixon line was fixed as the proper border (the Mason was Charles, the surveyor, not related to George, the lawmaker). Colonel Mason now also used his knowledge of land legislation to shape the proposed cession of western lands to the United States—a sore point holding up ratification of the Articles of Confederation among the states.

Mason's workday energy was prodigious, and it is little wonder that his colleagues marveled at his stamina. Hoping the western land problem might soon be solved, he confided to a friend that he was "anxious to do this last piece of service to the American Union, before I quit the Assembly, which I am determined to do at the end of the next session." He missed the crucial vote on the western cession act, however, giving as an excuse not the gout, which was bad enough, but "a conviction that I was no longer able to do any essential service." All he wanted, Mason kept insisting, was to spend the remainder of his life "in quiet & retirement."

The buildup of British military activity in the South that coincided with sporadic and unnerving naval raids along the Virginia coast heightened his apprehensions and denied him a chance to retire peacefully. In a particularly dark hour, when rumors were spawned and spread daily by the probability of defeat, Mason wrote his friends in the Continental Congress, passing along "a general opinion prevailing that our allies [the French] are spinning out the war in order to weaken America as well as Great Britain." He pleaded for a show of French naval strength as British landing parties burned warehouses and plundered estates dangerously close to Gunston Hall. With each rumor of British raiders he packed his family and sped inland, to return when the alarms proved false.

Though he had no way of knowing it in the summer of 1781 the curtain was about to drop on both his pessimistic predictions and the main British army. In one of those odd moments in the history of warfare, when fate's back is turned and strategy works precisely as planned, the French fleet that Mason despaired of ever seeing suddenly appeared on the broad York River. Completely besieged, Cornwallis surrendered, and for practical purposes the Revolution as a military event ended. Happily spared from the pillaging hands of redcoats, Gunston Hall was in Mason's eyes now to be the retreat from that public life and confusion he had found so wearisome.

And so it might have been, had not the problems of peace been even more perplexing than those created by war. Mason had been too involved, his advice too valuable, for friends who remained politically active to forget the quality of his services. Crisis after crisis appeared. The bonds of union had stood the test of war fairly well, but the pressure of a common emergency that had tightened them in 1775 disappeared even before the treaty of peace in 1783. Creeping disunity was becoming painful to watch. Mason, seeing it, was quite willing to pass along advice to Thomas Jefferson and other old friends, admitting to his son that he still liked to "dabble a little in politics" but disavowing any ambition to leave Fairfax County.

Although the role of elder statesman appealed to him, he was now to learn that personal aloofness robbed his advice of authority. Public men were not going to court favor or accept the counsel of a politically inactive Mason. Accordingly, he began to change his adamant stand. Early in 1783 he told Patrick Henry that bad men and bad measures had forced him from the Assembly, but hinted that with "tolerable health" he might return to the political battles. The attempt being made to cancel prewar debts owed to British merchants was just the type of legislation to stick firmly in his craw. The war, he said testily, had not been fought "to avoid our just debts or to cheat our creditors." Any effort to pass laws that would relieve Virginians of their old obligations was insolent, not to say dishonest. The sorry state of public credit and the worthlessness of paper currency compounded the offense. When the distinction was as clear as this between self-interest and fraud, Mason was quick to point it out.

More concerned with the state of affairs in Virginia than in the Union, he demanded fiscal soundness for the commonwealth while denying the right of the Continental Congress to levy any taxes. The feeble Congress, struggling with the old quota system of revenues (which meant practically no revenue, as states usually failed to meet or sometimes even to contribute at all to their share of national expenses), had asked vainly for approval of power to tax imports. Mason, far from alone in his fear of the potential power of Congress, foresaw one tax leading to another, then to the creation of an agency to enforce collection, perhaps an army. That the Congress was having to borrow from Peter to pay Paul and

JAMES MADISON *split with Mason and Patrick Henry over ratification of the Constitution, but later led the fight for adding to it the first ten amendments, known as the Bill of Rights.*

getting deeper into debt all the while did not especially concern him. The alternative did. Put the purse and the sword in the same hand, he said, and you would see an end to liberty.

It was a knotty issue, one that lay at the very heart of the problem: whether the new country was to be a mere league of adjacent states or whether those states would be willing, however timidly at first, to trade a measure of individual sovereignty for the promise of greater national strength. In each of the thirteen states men were jealous of their local powers, convinced that any grant of authority to the national legislature would cause untold mischief. Yet who would pay the foreign debt of the United States held by the French and Dutch bankers? Who would pay the domestic debt that had built up during the war? In these embarrassed circumstances Congress made a futile plea for some more efficient way of raising money. Time and again the states (any one state voting against a plan would kill it) said no.

From the vantage point of his seat in Congress, James Madison saw that the problem turned on the proper division of state and national powers. Madison was willing to yield state rights for overall strength. Mason reportedly thought that minor concessions would chip away the substance of state sovereignty and create an awkward behemoth. When Madison returned home late in 1783 he stopped at Gunston Hall to learn Mason's views firsthand. He then found Mason willing to discuss and consider favorably a national tax and other matters that Madison feared might arouse Mason's ire. "His heterodoxy lay chiefly in being too little impressed with either the necessity or the proper means of preserving the Confederacy," Madison wrote. It was a revealing analysis of Mason's establishment of political priorities: Virginia first, then the South, then the Union.

Such an attitude is to some degree more understandable in view of Mason's record of past public service. Never having served the public outside Virginia, he was inclined to see each measure and every policy from a point of view purely Virginian. In so doing, he developed a shortsightedness about national affairs that reinforced his unwavering loyalty to his native state. At the same time, his attitude also denied him a much larger place in national affairs and a more conspicuous role in our history.

Still he relished the position of behind-the-scenes adviser and balked at new efforts in 1784 to send him to the Assembly. On the eve of the attempt, Mason wrote to Martin Cockburn that unsolicited election would be "an oppressive and unjust invasion of my personal liberty."

Jefferson had hoped that pending land office legislation would lure Mason back to Richmond if anything would, but even that matter so dear to Mason's heart and interests could not budge his determination. When, however, the legislators proceeded to appoint him one of the state's delegation to arbitrate with Maryland commissioners the problem of navigation of the Potomac, he must have shrugged his shoulders and consoled himself with the thought that the work would be close to home. At any rate he took the assignment and went about it diligently until the first conference proved that more meetings were necessary. The variety of questions raised led to the call for the Annapolis Convention of 1786. Mason was appointed to serve there, too, but like most of the other delegates named he failed to attend.

The failure to get the Annapolis conference under way was to result in the call for a Federal Convention. The states were urged to appoint deputies to meet in Philadelphia the following spring in order to make the Articles of Confederation "adequate to the exigencies of the Union."

The most dramatic of the events in Virginia politics that preceded the Philadelphia meeting was an attempt to pass an Assembly bill providing for state-supported "Teachers of the Christian Religion." Mason joined with Madison and other liberals to defeat the plan by maneuvering its powerful advocate—Patrick

Henry—out of the Assembly and into the ineffectual position of governor. The brief campaign, highlighted by widespread distribution of Madison's *Remonstrance* assailing the idea of a general tax assessment for the support of religious instruction, again stirred up sentiment for complete freedom of religion and eased the way for the celebrated bill that finally established it in 1786.

In that year the states chose delegations for the coming Federal Convention—and with a good deal more discretion than they had been showing in their Congressional appointments. George Washington's name headed the Virginia list, followed by the new governor, Edmund Randolph, and by Henry, Madison, Mason, John Blair, and George Wythe. When Henry obstinately chose not to accept his commission, James McClurg was picked to replace the old warhorse of the statehouse.

Washington and Madison were ready to go further than the rest of the Virginians in surrendering some state prerogatives for national unity and strength. The original Convention plan simply called for an amendment of the Confederation system so that the United States might through Congress regulate commerce, restore public credit, and provide for the common defense of the Union. Washington spoke for the majority view when he wrote to Madison about his fears that the gains of the Revolution might be wiped away momentarily, since "we are fast verging to anarchy and confusion!" Washington was not in the habit of tossing exclamation points around recklessly. Daniel Shays's rebellious uprising in Massachusetts had been an unmistakable warning of the national temper.

Madison may not have shared such an extreme view, but he knew that the poor attendance record of Congress was but another symptom of the pitiful weakness of the Confederation. National panic might well have been lurking more prominently in the shadows than Madison realized. As mobs defied tax-collecting sheriffs, as farm produce rotted, seamen milled about idly on the docks, and commerce was everywhere enfeebled, men of wealth and political influence in most of the states called aloud for a government, as they said, "with energy." By energy they meant a strong national government that would take over some of the former state functions (for example, national administration of tariffs), stabilize the currency, and establish a federal military force. These things would cost money, but influential leaders realized that paying taxes would be preferable to the wobbly course of the Confederation. If surgery did not replace medication, the patient might soon die.

Would Mason join the general hue and cry for energetic government? Madison wished to know definitely, but he had to settle for rumors. To Jefferson, now minister to France, Madison reported that he had heard Mason was "renouncing his errors" regarding the Confederation "and means to take an active part in the amendment of it." The events of the next few months proved the rumor at least partially reliable.

CHAPTER SIX

Constitution and Compromise

BY the spring of 1787 the political apparatus of the young
United States government was operating at a level of dismal
inefficiency. Disabled from the start by the lack of taxing and
regulatory authority, the Articles of Confederation were further
enfeebled by the powerful reversion to self-interest that set in
among the new states after the peace. Practically, the Articles were
almost useless. Ostensibly they were to be overhauled at Philadelphia. But most of the delegates elected to participate in that process were going to the Quaker City as designers, not as repairmen.

No sooner did the Convention assemble than suggestive hints
and rumors began to drift out of Philadelphia that an entirely
new federal constitution was in the works. Among the delegates
waiting around for Mason and other latecomers to fill out a
quorum there was lively conversation about a two-branch legislature proportionately representing the population, a national

executive (instead of the powerless president of the Congress), and some means of subordinating state laws that conflicted with the national interest—perhaps a federal judiciary. Clearly the defects of the old Confederation had finally served a useful end by defining a system that would *not* work; on the other hand, those governments set up by the individual states showed signs of stability in the face of national weakness. What more reasonable than to pattern a national government on such plans as had already been followed in the states?

George Mason would perhaps be stunned, but not particularly shaken by these developments. At the moment he was traveling northward from Gunston Hall at a leisurely pace. At Baltimore he stopped over with friends and discussed with them their idea of "energetic government." Predictably the last of the Virginians to arrive, he alighted at the Indian Queen Tavern on May 17. One of the small, elegant apartments that had given the Inn its reputation was waiting for him and his son John.

A few days on the scene and Mason lost some of his apprehension about a drastic revision of the old system. Closeted with fellow deputies he began to feel that the "hopes of all the Union centre in this Convention." Furthermore, the magnitude of the undertaking was proving to be much more impressive than when he had viewed it from the south bank of the Potomac. He saw the domestic crisis with greater alarm than ever before, but one fact kept his pessimism in check: the caliber of various delegates held out the promise of sound thinking, a quality he had found conspicuously rare in his public career. He was surprised to find the northern deputies somewhat anti-republican, but explained this "extraordinary phenomenon" by saying that they had been the first zealots for popular government and were now "tired and disgusted with the unexpected evils they have experienced." Mason only hoped the Convention would not swing too far in the other direction.

By May 26 enough deputies were on hand to commence the business in earnest. To no one's surprise, Washington was unanimously chosen president of the assembly, and formal debate began.

A caucus of the Virginia delegation, under Madison's informal leadership, had already outlined a plan that Edmund Randolph lost no time in offering to the Convention. Fundamental to its scheme of separate legislative, executive, and judicial departments of government was representation according to population. The people would elect a lower house that would in turn elect an upper. Together the two houses would elect an executive and judges. It was smooth, premeditated strategy by the men from the Old Dominion, but the smaller states promptly sensed in it a pernicious move to gain control of the government. Under the Confederation they had held equal power in the Congress, and a single state could block any legislation. The Virginia plan would so obviously have given them a second-class status that deputies from some of the smaller states were miffed to the point of threatening to go home at once. (Rhode Island did not face that decision because she had refused to send delegates in the first place.)

Mason himself wanted the large states to hold the upper hand in the new government, though he did not feel that smaller states should bend the knee. To him the first consideration was to insure popular election of representatives to the larger house. The people, whether from states large or small, could always determine where their own interests lay. While he was quick to admit that "we had been too democratic" in the first flush of independence, he also feared that "we should incautiously run into the opposite extreme" by curbing the power of the individual voter. Elsewhere within the structure of government group interests could be accommodated, but only popular representation would protect those who stood to have no champion other than their elected delegate.

Elbridge Gerry of Massachusetts, the name of Daniel Shays still fresh in his memory, warned of the dangers of this "levilling spirit," but Mason gave no sign of disowning the Virginia Declaration of Rights. The Confederation allowed state legislatures to call the turn in national affairs; now he perceived, quite correctly, that changes being proposed would affect citizens more directly than ever before. That "all power is vested in, and consequently derived from, the people" moved him even to consider supporting popular elections for president, an advanced suggestion that he made no further show of favoring when it grew obvious that most of the Convention was appalled by it.

At the time, the public knew little of what was going on behind the doors of the Pennsylvania State House because the sessions were held without spectators present. Mason explained that to allow scattered leaks would expose "several crude and indigested parts" of a constitution that in the end might have a different complexion. The business should not be misrepresented by feeding piecemeal information to the public. Although this covenant was not to be openly arrived at, news got out anyway that the larger delegations were supporting Randolph's plan and that the smaller states had made a counterproposal for representation by states rather than by population. Breaking this deadlock became one of the major turning points of the Convention.

The compromise provided a lower house based on population and an upper house where states would be on an equal footing. This tallied with Mason's ideas as long as the lower chamber, representing a larger share of power for the bigger states, kept the exclusive right to originate laws involving money. Fearful of a future that might well see an ambitious president in league with a servile senate, he reflected the gnawing apprehension of Englishmen who for centuries had labored to keep purse and sword out of the same hands.

State legislators would pick the senators (which they in fact did until 1913), thus leaving the upper house in control of the states. Mason approved of that, opposed permitting Congress to disallow acts of state legislatures, and joined the vigorous debate on minimum ages for congressmen. He remembered that when he was twenty-one his political opinions had been notable chiefly for their immaturity. When someone suggested that Congress would prove to be a good school for young men, he retorted that this might be so but he "chose that they should bear the expense of their own education."

A few days of strenuous debate and Mason's old self began to show through. He soon complained of the "etiquette and nonsense so fashionable" in Philadelphia and wearily speculated that he might have to endure a month of it before the Convention finished its assignment. The only breaks in the serious business came in the evenings when the Indian Queen cooks outdid themselves, setting out their feasts amid table service that was, one record puts it, "in the style of noblemen."

Vestigial signs of royalty apparently could still be allowed on the dinner table. Mason's indulgence in the rich food and Madeira may have been controlled by the specter of gout, since he said little of his affliction during those days. He was a faithful attendant at the sessions, speaking to the point on practically every topic of importance. Much later Madison recalled that Mason bore himself well as "a powerful reasoner, a profound statesman, and a devoted Republican."

It was a judgment softened by time. In the thick of debate the two Virginians tilted with each other over a pet project of Mason's: a year's ineligibility to public appointment for congressmen whose terms were expiring. Mason scrambled a metaphor to call this a "corner stone in the fabric," holding that without such a ban corruption would become rampant. Madison conceded that in Virginia favors had been shown to former lawmakers, but he appealed to Mason "to vouch another fact not less notorious in Virginia, that the backwardness of the best citizens to engage in the legislative service gave but too great success to unfit characters."

The remark hit close home for Mason, its obvious target. Madison probably further strained the friendship when a short time later, in discussing the amending process, he observed that the defects of the Virginia Constitution were "evident to every person," but they could not succeed in amending it. Constitutionalist George Mason must have swallowed hard again.

As a counterbalance to his avowed republicanism, Mason unsuccessfully sought to set up a property qualification for Senate membership that would have given that body a distinctly aristocratic tone. He served on the committee that ironed out most of the lumps in the congressional representation clauses and finally admitted that some concessions there and elsewhere were vital. One of the lumps was a mountain that had to be reduced to a molehill—the ponderous slavery issue. If the number of representatives to be assigned to a state were to depend upon its population, were slaves to count as people or as property? The question generated new emotional peaks on the Convention floor and for Mason pitted his conscience against his sectional loyalty. Because counting slaves as freemen would add to the number of southern congressmen, delegates from the deeper South favored that plan; but to recognize slaves as free for that purpose *only* would seem to be tacit approval of slavery as a system. Mason made up his mind and threatened to leave the deliberations if the plan was carried for including slaves in the calculations. It did not carry completely, but the ratio of determining representation by counting three slaves for every five freemen did. The three-fifths rule kept him in Philadelphia.

His altruistic feeling that slavery was an inhuman device was well known in Virginia circles, but so were his extensive slave holdings common knowledge to the rest of the Convention. Aware of the contradiction, Mason moved to the sidelines. South Carolina, leading the skirmish to prohibit abolition of the slave trade, found enough Northern allies, at a price, for a compromise that would prohibit the importation of slaves for another twenty years.

Mason was nettled by the North-South coalition on the slavery issue because it weakened his hand on another sectional squabble. Like Madison, he saw great danger to the Union in the opposing interests of North and South. He therefore wanted a commitment from the Northern maritime states that southern products would not be taxed as exports. Aiming his remarks directly at the New England deputies, he said he hoped the North did not intend to deny this assurance to southern agriculture. The point was well made, and won; but to Mason it was but half the battle.

The crucial sectional issue then turned upon the license northern businessmen would have, with but a simple majority in Congress, actually to regulate southern commerce. (Mason had previously suggested a triple-headed presidency to hold North-Middle-South interests in balance, but the idea did not impress the delegates.) He feared that laws similar to those British regulatory measures that had been so obnoxious might again be passed, giving northern shippers an economic strangle hold on southern planters. The New Englanders were already pressing for such power. They had bargained for it at the price of their silence on slavery. The bill now fell due, and the lower South refused to back Mason and Randolph on the necessity of a two-thirds majority for the passage of commercial regulations by Congress. So bitterly did Mason feel the injustice of a simple majority vote that he warned it would deliver the southern states "bound hand & foot to the Eastern states, and enable them to exclaim, in the words of Cromwell on a certain occasion—'the Lord hath delivered them into our hands.'" Classing the North as an enemy, as Mason did here, betrayed a bias that the lower South might have shared if compromise had not been the order of the day.

This North-South compact angered Mason and caused him to drop his reticence on the slavery issue. Late in August he joined the few northern critics who were denouncing the slave traffic and lamented that New Englanders had "from a lust of gain embarked on this nefarious" business. He indirectly indicted himself by declaring that every master of slaves was a petty tyrant and warned that slavery would in time "bring the judgment of heaven on a country. As nations cannot be rewarded or punished in the next world they must be in this . . . Providence punishes national sins, by national calamities." As a prophet he had the weight of history on his side, but as a persuader of fellow deputies he gained little more than the sarcastic retort of Connecticut-bred Oliver Ellsworth. Never having owned a slave, Ellsworth said, he would not know how it affected a man's character, but if morals were the concern of the Convention they could go the limit and free all slaves, which were multiplying especially fast in Maryland and Virginia. For such a thrust Mason had no answer. He avoided the subject after that encounter, and the ban on Congressional interference with slavery for the next twenty years remained intact.

In the final sessions Mason carried his point on some of the minor issues but lost on nearly all the big ones. He wanted a council created to advise the president because of the immense concentration of power that potentially lay in the presidency. This warning his colleagues ignored. He thought the Constitution as worded would carry the implicit promise to redeem depreciated government obligations at par and would "beget speculations and increase the pestilent practice of stock-jobbing." On that score he was right, but his fellow delegates were deaf to Mason's plea for a toned-down statement. Then Mason turned to the procedure for amending the Constitution. This he found unacceptable and predicted that proper amendments would never be obtained "if the government should become oppressive, as he verily believed would be the case." Sharing the eighteenth-century preference for militia instead of mercenaries, Mason also wanted a prohibition on standing armies in time of peace but got nowhere with that proposal.

His victories in the concluding days of the Convention came

with the final decision to allow only the House of Representatives to originate appropriation bills, and with phraseology that implied curbs on the presidency. He wanted to persuade the deputies to add "maladministration" as a cause for the president's impeachment, but settled for his own alteration of "other high crimes & misdemeanors against the United States." Mason's criticism of the amending process probably led to the final version that seemingly gave the states more strength. But he became increasingly convinced that Virginia was giving up too much and gaining too little.

The most severe opposition to the Constitution did not take definite shape until the eleventh hour.

Gerry of Massachusetts, Mason, and Governor Randolph of Virginia made up the trio of dissidents. On September 12 Gerry and Mason started an attack on the failure to include a jury system in the judicial provisions and carried it to the point of moving that a bill of rights covering all such points be appended to the final draft. "A general principle" on jury trials and a few other matters would satisfy them, Mason explained, and would "give great quiet to the people." By using the state declarations, he modestly concluded, "a bill might be prepared in a few hours."

The suggestion for a bill of rights found no support. A New England deputy pointed out that the Constitution did not repeal the state declarations of rights, which adequately safeguarded the citizens' rights. Mason replied that the Constitution was to be the supreme law of the land, "paramount to the state bills of rights." No matter, said the other delegates, and neither Mason nor Gerry could muster a single state delegation in their support. How the leaders of the Federalist juggernaut would regret their haste in rejecting this idea!

Plainly, however, Mason and his two critical cohorts were now out of step with the Convention. They had in effect said that they would not support the Constitution unless vital issues were solved to their satisfaction. The desired concessions had not been made. Practical politics demanded, on the other hand, that the Constitution be sent to the people as a unified effort approved whole-heartedly by its draftsmen.

To meet this last challenge, Gouverneur Morris worded the signatory clause with the careful phrase, "unanimous consent of the states present," as a device that would even allow critics to sign though individually they could still oppose the plan. "We are not likely to gain many converts by the ambiguity," said General Pinckney of South Carolina, and he was right. Franklin made some remarks about the need for unanimity which the touchy Gerry resented. The Yankee deputy even threw out the veiled hint that a civil war was in the offing. The Constitution, Gerry said, would do nothing to stem the tide of anarchy. Randolph reported that he could not sign a constitution presented to the people on a platter with a this-or-nothing label.

Washington signed the engrossed copy and the other delegates —some of them since known to history by little beyond this one act—awaited their turn. Mason, even if he was present, sat on his hands and refused to sign.

One of the great power struggles in American political history began on this discordant note. In the Continental Congress, where the Constitution was sent for transmittal to the states, a faction led by Richard Henry Lee tried to add a bill of rights to the plan. The move failed, but with some trepidation the friends of the Constitution guided it through the Congress; the skirmishes there were a prelude to larger battles already being planned elsewhere.

"Col. Mason left Philada. in an exceeding ill humour indeed," Madison recorded. Before he took leave of the City of Brotherly Love, however, Mason met with local politicians who agreed with him that the Convention had added to, rather than solved, their problems. He must have then showed them the list of objections he had scribbled on the blank portions of the printed final committee report. They began with the powerful charge: there is no Declaration of Rights. Therein lay the principal weakness in the new governmental machinery—adequate power, but uncertain control of it. The president would in time become "a tool of the Senate" or else a cabinet would spring up to guide the government, a cabinet that might well "be induced to join in any dangerous or oppressive measures, to shelter themselves, and prevent an inquiry into their own misconduct in office." Mason was equally certain that a federal judiciary would destroy state courts and make legal action "tedious, intricate & expensive . . . enabling the rich to oppress & ruin the poor." Commercial monopolies favoring the North would appear if the Constitution were to be ratified. There was an ominous final judgment: the Constitution in operation would begin with a moderate aristocracy and eventually turn into an outright monarchy, or at least "a corrupt oppressive aristocracy; it will most probably vibrate some years between the two, and then terminate in the one or the other."

Not without plan, Mason's arguments rapidly found their way into print. Along the entire seaboard opponents of ratification (labeled "Antifederalists" by their enemies, and the name stuck). were soon distributing them in the form of a pamphlet called *Objections to the Constitution*. It was one of their handbooks. By Christmas, 1787, the polemic was being denounced by Federalists everywhere as the vitriolic ravings of a bitter old man.

Rebuffed and angry, Mason left for Virginia in the company of James McHenry of Maryland. As they rode they argued the pros and cons of the Constitution bump by bump, for McHenry had decided to support it. When they neared Baltimore, a reporter wrote, Mason's "charioteer put an end to the dispute, by jumbling their Honors together by an oversett . . . they were both hurt—the Col. most so—he lost blood at Baltimore—& is well."

CHAPTER SEVEN

The Antifederalist Crusade

THE distressing outcome of four sultry months in Philadelphia, amplified by the accident and bloodletting in Maryland, was the climax of an adventure that left Mason in a truculent mood by the time he reached Gunston Hall. More disheartening still was the prospect of further acrimonious debate ahead. He was no stranger to an unpopular cause, but this time there was a formidable difference: the opposition included most of those who formerly had been on his side. Yet the likelihood that old friendships might founder on the shoals of ratification deterred him not at all. He promptly opened a correspondence with Richard Henry Lee aimed at coordinating strategy to defeat the Constitution. Almost as promptly Washington got wind of the alliance and bitterly pointed to Lee as the master of their plotting.

At the meeting of the Assembly in Richmond, Washington expected Mason to vote in favor of an act calling for a ratifying convention, but feared that he might also use that occasion to parade frightening, and possibly persuasive, objections. "To alarm the people seems to be the ground work of his plan," he wrote, and the atmosphere between the two old friends began to chill even before Mason left for Richmond.

The Assembly that opened in October, 1787 was to be Mason's last as a member of the House of Delegates. By the time he arrived (late) it was known to the entire legislature that George Mason was set to fight adoption of the Constitution. Likewise Patrick Henry, who had turned down a seat in the Philadelphia Convention because, he later claimed, he had "smelt a rat" in its proceedings.

Much of the work of inspiring the company of Virginia Antifederalists fell on Henry's shoulders. He and Mason pushed through the General Assembly a bill for a ratifying convention that carried an explicit recommendation for a second federal convention to consider amendments put forward by the states, and they urged cooperation of the states to carry out such a design. Governor Edmund Randolph, his Antifederalism much cooler than it had been at Philadelphia, thwarted the latter part of the plan. Sparring for time, Mason and Henry wanted the Virginia convention held at the last possible moment. It was set for June, 1788, in a move that Federalists considered almost indecent for its obvious tardiness. Let other, and smaller, states contend for the honor of being early adherents to the Constitution.* By June it would be apparent to the Federalists that the Constitution could not be enacted without protective amendments. Such was the strategy.

There was other business that autumn and winter for the Virginia Assembly. Throughout the course of it Mason must have been aware that his voice was less forceful in counsel, that among

---

* By mid-January, 1788, five of them had ratified: Delaware, Pennsylvania, New Jersey, Georgia, and Connecticut.

close friends his opposition to the Constitution was producing a disfavor that found expression in courteous but unmistakable ways, that he was now more often being indulged than applauded. The British debt question that came up again found him taking the same stand as before, but this time no converts came to sit beside him on the issue.

One member wrote to Madison in the Continental Congress that the Colonel's arguments against taxes on imports "were vague & inconclusive in short altho he is sometimes much admired for great strength of mind originality of expression & for the comprehensive view which he takes of his subjects yet upon that occasion he fell far short of the general expectation, & I fear the effects of age have sometimes been discoverable in him." At times Mason was his old brilliant self in the House, but there were also times when weariness and age showed through all too plainly. Out of such reports later came the story that when Mason campaigned in Stafford County for a seat at the ratifying convention (Fairfax freeholders were solid Federalists, and he knew he would stand no chance in his home county), his opponent declared it well known to the public that the Colonel's mind was failing. "Sir," replied Mason, "when yours fails nobody will ever discover it."

To the north, Antifederalists were showing occasional spurts of strength. In New Hampshire they held a majority in the first convention but the instructed delegates, charged by constituents to vote "no," were persuaded to adjourn for a second consideration in the spring. In neighboring Massachusetts, the majority of farmers and back-country delegates, generally opposed to the Constitution, were easily outmaneuvered in debate by skilled Federalist lawyers. Gerry was humiliated to the point that he stalked out of the Boston convention where he had been an invited guest. Contested seats went to Federalists, dark whispers of bribery were brushed aside, and early in February the Massachusetts convention voted 187-168 in favor of the Constitution. The sudden appearance of popular Governor Hancock with a set of recommendatory amendments under his arm had done the trick.

While the Federalists considered the outcome in Massachusetts crucial, they did not rest on that victory. Elsewhere they pushed the attack with tradesmen's rallies, newspaper philippics, and other arts of persuasion that politicians practiced then as now. The Antifederalists lacked leadership, despite their numbers, and when they did issue an anti-Constitution tract such as Mason's *Objections* they omitted in their northern edition his blast at the power to regulate commerce, an omission the Federalists gleefully corrected.

In March, 1788, the Rhode Island citizens rejected the Constitution at the polls instead of in convention. It was the only test made in such a forthright manner: all the other states followed the recommended convention plan for ratification. When sister southern states Maryland and South Carolina ratified by comfortable margins, Virginia Federalists forgot Rhode Island and cheered loudly for the eight states already in the Federal procession. Only one more was needed. In a desperate effort to hold the line Mason and Henry opened a correspondence with the Federal-Republican committee in New York that was making a last-ditch stand; their faint hope was to coordinate Antifederal plans in the two key states. The Virginians had agreed to try to force another federal convention but were kept ignorant of Governor Clinton's implied approval of such a move by Governor Randolph's failure to relay the letter. When he finally did release it, and it was too late to do anything in concert, Mason denounced in violent terms such "duplicity." The effect the letter might have had was forever lost.

As the day neared for the crack of the gavel opening the Virginia convention Federalist fire was aimed mainly at Mason. Federalists would have found Patrick Henry a bigger target, but

the chinks in his armor were few. Their strategy was to discredit
Mason by giving prominence to every incident that might prove
the master of Gunston Hall no longer the luminary in Virginia
politics he had been for so many years. In pamphlets they charged
that Mason's list of objections were simply his afterthoughts, re-
vised by Richard Henry Lee "and by him brought into their
present artful and insidious form." They circulated copies of
Oliver Ellsworth's "Landholder" essays which held that opposition
in Virginia came from two sources—"the madness of Mason, and
the enmity of the Lee faction to General Washington." Invective
was seldom tempered with charity, though one critic in a Richmond newspaper dropped the remark into his attack that Mason's
mental powers were still vigorous and his acts based on a concept
of what was right, not what was popular. Faint praise, if not the
damning kind. Federalists meeting for their second convention
in New Hampshire lined up Mason and Henry with the local opposition and let go their volleys. Arch-federalist Nicholas Gilman
thought the Virginians were confounding the hopes of honest
men everywhere. "Had it been pleasing to the preserver of man,"
said Gilman, to have removed them "to the regions of darkness,
I am induced to think the new system of government would have
been adopted" speedily.

The national spotlight, however, was on the Virginia convention. It assembled in the Academy recently erected on Shockoe
Hill in Richmond, a building large enough to hold both the
elected delegates and a throng of spectators. The June air was full
of rumors, of courting the undecided, of lobbying for the votes
of the Kentuckians, who in preliminary surveys appeared to hold
the balance of power. William Grayson, Mason's friend from
Dumfries, enlisted as a strong Antifederalist; but Richard Henry
Lee, a valuable ally, had failed to stand for a convention seat.
Madison, Edmund Pendleton, and other powerful Federalists
found that the wavering Randolph had finally joined their cause.

It was only a mild surprise. A greater one awaited them when Mason moved that the Constitution be debated clause by clause, a maneuver that Federalists, sensing the danger of a quick vote, secretly began to hope would promote their own cause.

Preliminary skirmishing out of the way, the giants on each side of the house began to unlimber heavier artillery. Henry launched his attack on the Constitution as a usurpation of the powers of the federal convention, while Randolph replied with a plea for a union that rose above the individual areas of conflict. Mason charged that the power of the federal government to levy taxes would destroy the state governments and insisted that amendments must be made before Virginia ratified. Madison urged Mason to consider the Constitution more carefully, that he might discover errors in his logic. Then Madison dashed off a note to Washington, who anxiously awaited some news, reporting that Henry and Mason "made a lame figure" in the debates and "appeared to take different and awkward ground." The Federalists were concentrating on winning the Kentucky delegates, Madison added, "and every piece of address is going on privately to work on the local interests and prejudices of that and other quarters."

The delegates from Kentucky, Virginia's westernmost county, held high trumps in the game. The right to ship products down the Spanish-owned Mississippi River was their chief interest; their votes would be had for the promise of receiving that privilege. The North was indifferent to the problem. Federalists could hardly have been less eager to jump into a quarrel with Spain by guaranteeing something they had no control over. George Mason, with his ready knowledge of the West, knew that. Therefore it was merely a matter of tactics to play on the Kentuckian's fears that Federalists would actually oppose use of the river. Critical votes rode on how delicately, how convincingly that could be done. In the cumbersome trade negotiations with the Spanish, certain northerners (now arch-Federalists) had been willing to swap the

Mississippi waterway for a promised market for their products. Madison viewed the Kentucky delegates as safely Federal at first, "but the torch of discord has been thrown in and has found the materials but too inflammable." With the rest of the state almost evenly divided, the Mississippi issue seemed ready-made for Patrick Henry's calculated persuasiveness. "Mr. Henry, whose opinions have their usual influence, has been heard to say that he would rather part with the confederation than relinquish the navigation of the Mississippi," Federalist John Marshall warned.

Henry would hold the gallery and delegates spellbound for a whole day, playing on the fears of the western counties and declaring that without a bill of rights the whole Constitution had the stamp of suspicion upon it. Randolph would follow, trying to refute Henry point by point. Mason then would take up the Antifederalist chant, and Grayson or young James Monroe stood by to relieve the two chieftains. John Marshall, James Innes, and other young men assisted Madison and Randolph, but the Federalists remained on the defensive. Repeatedly the Henry-Mason coalition brought forward wholesale charges that had become Antifederalist dogma. They ranged from criticism that the wording was loose and the Constitution too general to a warning that the nation was too large to be governed equitably by a federal system. On the last point rumors that Henry favored a southern confederacy rather than a union of all states seemed confirmed by the accusations he directed at the North.

Long convinced that the Federalists were delaying and pillaging their mail, the Antifederalists in Richmond had their letters sent to unsuspected addresses. Mason wrote the Antifederalist message center in New York that the Massachusetts amendments would furnish them a starting point, but stronger action would give the Virginians more ammunition. Henry was equally hopeful that by acting jointly Virginia and New York still could hold the ratification process in check and force another convention call.

Could a union exist without New York and Virginia? The absurdity of such a disjointed federation should be obvious enough to reasonable men.

The stakes were high and, while the tired author of the Virginia Declaration of Rights looked on, Henry slashed at the Federalists for their failure to include freedom of religion and the press in the Constitution. Hundreds of dissenters had already poured their fears into petitions that the delegates must have read, making it apparent that the silence in the Constitution on religious affairs had been construed as Mason had warned it might be —not as the Federalists had assumed it would. One by one, Henry pointed to other civil rights on which the Constitution stood strangely silent. He also brought out a letter from Jefferson—still in France—that gave the former governor's initial position on ratification. Withhold ratification until a bill of rights is added was Jefferson's advice (he later changed his mind in favor of the Massachusetts plan of recommending amendments). Henry made the most of it.

Mason took up the line and argued that if the people felt insecure in their liberties dreadful calamities must surely follow. The implied threat of a rebellion must have caused a shudder in the house. Light Horse Harry Lee rose to his feet to ask if Mason was not trying to bring about the very "horrors which he deprecates?" Lee then said he hoped "the madness of some, and the vice of others" would not bring on such an evil day in Virginia.

Tempers bristled. Henry hastened to assure the Federalists that they might have union and peace if they would only concede the necessity for some amendments to the Constitution *before* it was ratified. Then he produced a lengthy draft of proposed alterations, probably drawn up by Mason, that included a bill of rights and proposals to meet Antifederal objections the two men had spelled out during the preceding weeks. Mason listened to Randolph attack the amendments and then defended the proposal to

require more than a simple congressional majority for laws affect-
ing the regulation of commerce. He recalled the horse trading that
had won the northerners that concession, but argued that Randolph was wrong to assert the North would balk if the South
insisted on a two-thirds majority.

Madison, as perceptive a politician as ever stood up in debate,
saw that a critical juncture had been reached. He admitted that
some amendments might be acceptable to the Federalists, not that
they would be needed but simply to quiet some fears that had been
raised. However, these amendments would simply be recommended to the first Congress to consider. If Virginia insisted on
staying out of the Union by calling for amendments *prior* to
ratification, then Mason had been right in saying that evil days
lay ahead.

The tide was turning. Henry's hints that North Carolina and
New York would join in plans to upset ratification apparently
backfired, for there now came appeals for union. Young James
Innes made a masterful speech, recalling that the wartime victories had not been called Virginian or Carolinian, but by "the
glorious name of American . . . then beloved and confided in."
Innes spoke on, reaching eloquently for a new vision of America
that transcended localism, while the hushed gallery clung to
every word. When he finished even Henry was forced to call
Innes' remarks "splendid, magnificent and sufficient to shake the
human mind!"

Mason sat in silence through these scenes; and when Randolph
made his final speech of justification for his political about-face
Mason must have viewed the Governor with contemptuous resignation. Then the vote on Henry's motion for previous amendments began. No absolutely consistent pattern in the voting developed, but essentially the southern and western counties voted
Antifederal while the seaboard and Northern Neck went Federal.
The Henry-Mason maneuvers were defeated, 88 to 80.

No shouts of triumph came from the Federalists on June 25 when the result was known. The victory was too narrow, the opposition still too powerful, for an orgy of congratulation among the winners. The Constitution was then perfunctorily ratified by an 89-79 margin and, as a gesture of compromise, the Federalists joined in creating a committee, with Mason and Henry among its members, to prepare a list of recommendatory amendments. The list Henry had introduced became the basis of their report, including the stormy section on regulating commerce. But, as the Federalists frankly admitted, what was the harm now?

Mason was crushed. "The decision has been distressing & awful to great numbers of very respectable members," one of his friends recorded. A tired and beaten George Mason shuffled into his quarters at the Swan Tavern that night, closing what seemed to him a dark day in Virginia's history—certainly the darkest since the war.

Brooding over the event, he discussed the next step with Henry. They apparently decided to issue an Antifederalist manifesto similar to one that had come from dissenting elements at the Pennsylvania Convention. The Pennsylvanians had actually succeeded in calling a rump convention at Harrisburg that in September was to consider further means of making the Constitution palatable. Madison thought that neither Mason nor Henry meant to disturb the public peace with this enterprise, but publication of their reasons for dissenting "if it had not been defeated by the general moderation of the party, would probably have done mischief."

When the news from Richmond reached Poughkeepsie, New York, Federalists were already exultant: unknown to the Virginians on June 25, New Hampshire four days before had become the ninth state to ratify the Constitution. With the required majority behind the Constitution, ratification by New York in July and postponement by North Carolina at the same time were simply postscripts to a contest already ended. The United States of America now had a more potent, more "energetic" government. But if the Antifederalists were decisively beaten, their unanimity was far from shattered by the outcome. That would be obvious in the months ahead.

CHAPTER EIGHT

Retreat to Gunston Hall

THE discord at the ratifying convention left its scars. Colonel Mason now spoke of Edmund Randolph as "young A——d," comparing his former associate with the detested Benedict Arnold. Washington himself was in no mood for charity; he alluded to Mason as his "quondam friend." Troubled by the only significant defeat of his public career, Mason was further hurt by this coolness, though in truth both men suffered from the same political malady: intolerance of opponents and dark suspicion of their true motives. The Colonel justified his conduct of 1787-88 as springing "from the purest motives of honesty . . . and I would not forfeit the approbation of my own mind for the approbation of any man, or all the men upon earth." Presumably that included the General. Still it must have hurt Mason to see old friends turn the other way or to hear their hollow greetings.

Neglected business at Gunston Hall filled so much of his time that he had few moments to brood over the collapse of friendships. He stayed in Richmond only long enough to see the legislature rebuke Randolph for sitting on the letter from the governor of New York until Virginia's ratification made it meaningless. Back home, gout permitting, he mounted up each morning and rode out over the fields—it was midsummer now and tobacco was leafing out well—planning, directing, supervising the seasonal plantation program as he had since youth. The clap of a gavel, the pretentious and exaggerated courtesies of parliamentary exchange, off-the-floor plotting, subtle signs of personal ambition protruding from a delegate's otherwise well-concealed character: they seemed far away when all Mason could hear was the counterfeit call of the ubiquitous Virginia mockingbird, or the distant sound of a field hand debating a change of direction with his mule. Curious symbols those, if one chose to make them so.

To John, his homesick son in France, he sent one of the mockingbirds. All of the children, whom he described as "free from vices, good natured, obliging and dutiful," were now grown and gone from Gunston Hall, the sons to estates laid out by their father or to mercantile posts established with his help. The children reflected the care and good judgment under which they had come to maturity. No imprudent acts or lapses of integrity caused Mason to fear for their well-being. His lone apprehension was that his own career might end on a note of discord and failure, and indeed it would if the triumphant Federalists somehow broke the faith and recanted on their promise to add amendments to the Constitution. Mason watched, and waited.

The first news seemed more promising than he had expected. As a concession, Federalists in New York had agreed to a letter that would be circulated among the states, suggesting that the amendment proposals be made in a new federal convention. Virginia legislators were willing, but the plan proved to be an abortive effort when other states virtually ignored it. Federalist fears that it would "set everything afloat again" subsided, though not for long.

It was, in fact, becoming clear from indications throughout the new United States that the two parties who had engaged in a tug-of-war over the Constitution had by no means disbanded after the contest. The winners, ridiculed by some as "Non-Emendo-Tories," were given no time to relax by the losers, who were not going to lie down and play dead while the Constitution was still unamended. In Virginia, Antifederalists controlled the Assembly. Choice political plums went to friends, other honors to the right people—a new county in the Kentucky district was named Mason. Henry adroitly managed the legislature so that Antifederalists Richard Henry Lee and William Grayson were chosen the Virginia senators. Henry also recognized in undersized James Madison a political heavyweight to be kept out of the first Congress and pitted James Monroe against him. Madison won, but barely.

Madison fulfilled his campaign promise to secure a bill of rights. Mason's own 1776 design was a model and the Colonel viewed Madison's version with approval. "With two or three further amendments—such as confining the federal judiciary to admiralty & maritime jurisdiction," and the other repairs Mason had sought at the federal and state conventions—include those, he wrote, and "I could chearfully put my hand & heart to the new government." Meanwhile, Senator Grayson died and the seat was offered to Mason by Governor Beverley Randolph. The opportunity of joining his old friend Lee in the Senate must have tempted him, but in his sixty-fifth year he found it easier than before to resist the political call-to-arms.

During the next three years Mason was pleased to see many southern politicians adopt the position he had held in 1787: the Constitution took from the states more than it gave in return. The Judiciary Act of 1789 seemed to set up an all-powerful federal court system, a threat he had spotted and denounced as implicit in the Constitution. Hamilton's plan for funding the public debt appeared to favor northern business interests at the expense of southern farmers. Mason told Jefferson that Hamilton had "done us more injury than Great Britain and all her fleets and armies." And he never let go of his conviction that the convention compromise on slavery had placed a potential millstone around the neck of southern agriculture. Jefferson himself, his political philosophy firmly rooted in the soil, saw some remedy in increasing congressional representation from all the farming regions. Such testimonials implying Jefferson's continued friendship were especially welcome at Gunston Hall. So was the news that Madison was reading himself out of the Federalist party, and that he still regarded the Colonel with "undiminished . . . complete esteem."

Vindication of Mason's judgment came also from Richmond when the Assembly balked at ratifying the proposed federal Bill of Rights (on the ground that the articles were "far short of what the people of Virginia wish") and decried the effort to settle campaign pledges "with amendments so inadequate." In that frame of mind the Virginians withheld their approval until the Old Dominion became the last of the states necessary to ratify the Bill of Rights; that was done, as much from resignation as from conviction, on December 10, 1791.

Late in September, 1792, Jefferson stopped at Gunston Hall on his way to Philadelphia. He found Mason hobbling about on a crutch from attacks of gout that were now more frequent and lasting longer. Together the two old friends reviewed the crowded years since the summer of 1776. In spite of the gout and the fevers that had left him "weak and low" throughout the summer, Mason's memory was good, his manner still impeccably genteel, his convictions as vigorously asserted as they had been at Williamsburg. Only the coalition in Philadelphia that had bargained away any hope of eliminating slavery left a residue of disgust. For the rest, much had been gained. A man could go to sleep contented with the health of his new government, if not supremely happy about it. Like the universe divided by reason, a government divided by states leaves a remainder. And in each case that remainder must become the object of faith.

On Sunday afternoon, October 7, Colonel Mason surrendered up his faith to the safekeeping of others and died quietly in the home he had built with such meticulous affection thirty-five years before. Within sight of both Gunston Hall and the river, the family buried him "close by the side of my dear and ever lamented wife," his beloved Ann.

So came to an end the career, and the life, of this gifted Virginian "of the first order of greatness." Measured against any standard, it was a great career. At the start of the final quarter of the eighteenth century, Americans cast themselves adrift from the British Empire with only a single outstanding asset: the quality of their leadership. The special kind of leadership that George Mason brought to the critical problems of that critical age are worth some final comment.

The decision to revolt grew out of what Americans considered violations of the principles of government under which they and their grandfathers had been born. Whether violation was merely misinterpretation is arguable. If those principles had been written down as a constitution, which they were not, the result might have been the same. But at least it would have been harder, if not more embarrassing, for Parliament and George III to sidestep a written set of rules defining the relationship between themselves and the English people. On the threshold of revolt the American colonists set great store in justifying their acts and in stating their aims— on paper. The emergency, therefore, cried out as loudly for intellectual as for military talent. George Mason was one of the generals in the intellectual leadership of revolution.

The Virginia Declaration of Rights was more than a list of pertinent ideas embodied in clear and forceful phrases. The Declaration gave a handle to the thinking of the Revolutionary generation as the people sought to give substance and meaning to their effort to establish an independent existence as a nation. It was a statement of purpose, of intent, a moral commitment to a set of rules.

law. It was a guide to legality, to statutes that would be made enforceable by a constitution. It was the key to constitutional design, but it specified the character of the foundation without dictating the form of the structure that would sit upon it. Constitutions of the individual states, during the war years and after, proved themselves to be far better than mere stopgap instruments of government.

Not so with the document that controlled the relationship of the states through their representatives meeting together. The Articles of Confederation were a failure, though a failure that pinpointed a problem: how to achieve in a republic of states the proper balance between liberty and authority. The Articles demonstrated that too much undirected liberty could be as stifling and inefficient as an excess of authority. Hence it was clear that the common good called for redefining the role of the national government.

The debates on the Constitution represented a clash of doctrines that, as Alfred North Whitehead said, is not a disaster but an opportunity. It was a chance to argue out the problem of liberty versus authority. Mason's quarrel with the final form of the Constitution, far from reducing his stature as an intellectual leader, serves to confirm it.

Start with man himself, Mason might have put it. The best agent of a man's personal rights is himself. The next best is the community of interests of which he is a member. To it he delivers, by proxy of his vote, certain of his rights to be more effectively enjoyed in common with other men, as, for example, the protection of his property. But the greater the distance between a man and the control of his rights the more likely are they to invite infringement. This position was at the root of Mason's objections to the Constitution. A man's liberty needs more vigilant guardians than do his lands and chattels.

If the trusteeship of man's rights was to be more federal than local then there must be guarantees for their safety. These guarantees could not be left as unwritten, unrecorded assurances. Federalists might argue all they pleased that if the Constitution did not say anything about rights then it implied no control of them. That was not sufficient for the belligerent, unyielding master of Gunston Hall. He wanted it down in writing. He had appealed in vain, before the Revolution, to unwritten guarantees. No more of that.

By refusing to support the unamended Constitution, by doggedly defending local, state, and regional interests against the trading of too much liberty for too much authority, by steering shy of open political hassles except in line of duty to his beloved state of Virginia, Mason forfeited acclaim that history laid generously upon both his friends and his adversaries. His achievements as an intellectual leader, and as a consultant to other intellectual leaders, were obscured by the tumult of those final years.

Mason would have enjoyed the greater approbation of history; he was vain to that extent. But for years even his grave at Gunston Hall was unmarked and neglected. That was a detail of small moment. His greatest memorial was to be the Virginia Declaration of Rights. In that precursor of the federal Bill of Rights, he captured the spirit of his era—a vision that would in time spread over the land and cross oceans with a message of hope and human dignity. Withal, Mason was a man bound by contradictions: a slaveholder who hated slavery, a gifted politician who loathed petty politics, a gentleman who trusted the voice of the people. These inner clashes produced a reluctant statesman, but one who still was, as Jefferson believed, "of the first order of greatness."

G Mason

The Virginia Declaration of Rights

A DECLARATION of RIGHTS _made by the representatives of the good people of_ Virginia, _assembled in full and free Convention; which rights do pertain to them, and their posterity, as the basis and foundation of government._

1. That all men are by nature equally free and independent, and have certain inherent rights, of which, when they enter into a state of society, they cannot, by any compact, deprive or divest their posterity; namely, the enjoyment of life and liberty, with the means of acquiring and possessing property, and pursuing and obtaining happiness and safety.
2. That all power is vested in, and consequently derived from, the people; that magistrates are their trustees and servants, and at all times amenable to them.

111

3. That government is, or ought to be, instituted for the common benefit, protection, and security, of the people, nation, or community, of all the various modes and forms of government that is best, which is capable of producing the greatest degree of happiness and safety, and is most effectually secured against the danger of mal-administration; and that whenever any government shall be found inadequate or contrary to these purposes, a majority of the community hath an indubitable, unalienable, and indefeasible right, to reform, alter, or abolish it, in such manner as shall be judged most conducive to the publick weal.

4. That no man, or set of men, are entitled to exclusive or separate emoluments or privileges from the community, but in consideration of publick services; which, not being descendible, neither ought the offices of magistrate, legislator, or judge, to be hereditary.

5. That the legislative and executive powers of the state should be separate and distinct from the judiciary; and, that the members of the two first may be restrained from oppression, by feeling and participating the burthens of the people, they should, at fixed periods, be reduced to a private station, return into that body from which they were originally taken, and the vacancies be supplied by frequent, certain, and regular elections, in which all, or any part of the former members, to be again eligible, or ineligible, as the laws shall direct.

6. That elections of members to serve as representatives of the people, in assembly, ought to be free; and that all men, having sufficient evidence of permanent common interest with, and attachment to, the community, have the right of suffrage, and cannot be taxed or deprived of their property for publick uses without their own consent, or that of their representatives so elected, nor bound by any law to which they have not, in like manner, assented for the publick good.

7. That all power of suspending laws, or the execution of laws, by any authority without consent of the representatives of the people, is injurious to their rights, and ought not to be exercised.

8. That in all capital or criminal prosecutions a man hath a right to demand the cause and nature of his accusation, to be confronted with the accusers and witnesses, to call for evidence in his favour, and to a speedy trial by an impartial jury of his vicinage, without whose unanimous consent he cannot be found guilty, nor can he be compelled to give evidence against himself; that no man be deprived of his liberty except by the law of the land, or the judgment of his peers.

9. That excessive bail ought not to be required, nor excessive fines imposed, nor cruel and unusual punishments inflicted.

10. That general warrants, whereby any officer or messenger may be commanded to search suspected places without evidence of a fact committed, or to seize any person or persons not named, or whose offence is not particularly described and supported by evidence, are grievous and oppressive, and ought not to be granted.

11. That in controversies respecting property, and in suits between man and man, the ancient trial by jury is preferable to any other, and ought to be held sacred.

12. That the freedom of the press is one of the great bulwarks of liberty, and can never be restrained but by despotick governments.

13. That a well regulated militia, composed of the body of the people, trained to arms, is the proper, natural, and safe defence of a free state; that standing armies, in time of peace, should be avoided, as dangerous to liberty; and that, in all cases, the military should be under strict subordination to, and governed by, the civil power.

14. That the people have a right to uniform government; and therefore, that no government separate from, or independent of,

the government of *Virginia,* ought to be erected or established within the limits thereof.

15. That no free government, or the blessings of liberty, can be preserved to any people but by a firm adherence to justice, moderation, temperance, frugality, and virtue, and by frequent recurrence to fundamental principles.

16. That religion, or the duty which we owe to our CRE-ATOR, and the manner of discharging it, can be directed only by reason and conviction, not by force or violence; and therefore all men are equally entitled to the free exercise of religion, according to the dictates of conscience; and that it is the mutual duty of all to practise Christian forbearance, love, and charity, towards each other.

Beſt Virginia

A Note on the Sources

Scattered letters from George Mason's pen now rest in collections from Boston to Richmond, but the main body is gathered in the Mason papers at the Library of Congress. Helpful additions to this group are found at the Virginia State Library, and the Emmet Collection of the New York Public Library has been an immense aid. A considerable body of information was gathered by Kate Mason Rowland for her two-volume *Life of George Mason* . . . (New York, 1892), and many of her sources have somehow disappeared. The author's three-volume edition of *The Papers of George Mason* (Chapel Hill, 1970) includes many documents Miss Rowland overlooked. Helen Hill Miller's two books, *George Mason, Constitutionalist* (Cambridge, Mass., 1938) and *George Mason, Gentleman Revolutionary* (Chapel Hill, 1975), along with Pamela C. Copeland and Richard K. McMaster, *The Five George Masons* (Charlottesville, Va., 1975) are worthwhile secondary accounts that supplement manuscript discoveries with a combination of graceful writing and sound research. Mason's role in the Federal Convention is thoroughly covered in Max Farrand, ed., *The Records of the Federal Convention* (4 vols., New Haven, 1911–1937). His remarks in the Virginia Convention of 1788 are found in *Debates and Other Proceedings of the Convention in Virginia . . .* (Richmond, 1805). Unfortunately, the journals kept in the House of Burgesses and the House of Delegates reveal nothing regarding Mason's forensic ability or his intellect. A colorful, partisan, and often delightful view of Mason and his contemporaries is set down in Hugh Blair Grigsby's *The Virginia Convention of 1776* (Richmond, 1855) and *The Virginia Ratifying Convention of 1788* (2 vols., Richmond, 1890–1891).

The Virginia of Mason's day has been ably reconstructed by a number of outstanding historians. Noteworthy are Edmund S. Morgan's *Virginians at Home* (Williamsburg, 1952) and Douglas Southall Freeman's splendid chapter "Virginia During the Youth of Washington" in his first volume of *George Washington* (New York, 1948). Charles S. Sydnor's *Gentlemen Freeholders* (Chapel Hill, 1952) gives a lucid account of the political system that nurtured Mason and his contemporaries. A similar theme is developed in Dumas Malone's article, "The Great Generation," in the *Virginia Quarterly Review*, XXIII, No. 1, January, 1947, 108-122. R. R. Beirne and J. H. Scarff in *William Buckland, Architect of Virginia and Maryland* (Baltimore, 1958) include a chapter on Gunston Hall in their excellent survey of Buckland's short career.

Finally, there is much to be said for visual research. A visit to Gunston Hall, near Lorton, Virginia, is recommended for any reader who wishes to see George Mason's home, which remains intact after over two centuries as possibly the most attractive of all the colonial tidewater structures still standing.

FINE
Virginia Weed.

Acknowledgments

This book benefited immeasurably from the editorial hand of James R. Short of Colonial Williamsburg, who gave the manuscript a final polish at a critical moment. Generous research grants from the University of California, Los Angeles, and the American Philosophical Society aided in the research phase. Captain Walter Price, Jr., and the staff at Gunston Hall have been helpful at every turn. The Colonial Dames of America assisted my research and writing on George Mason for two decades. And I am indebted to the LSU Press and its skilled editors for their patience and their wisdom.

BeftVirginia.

Index

Lanterns on the Levee: Recollections of a Planter's Son
William Alexander Percy

Darwin and the Modern World View John C. Greene

Bricks Without Straw Albion W. Tourgée. Edited by Otto H. Olsen

The Barber of Natchez Edwin Adams Davis and
William Ransom Hogan

Bourbonism and Agrarian Protest: Louisiana Politics, 1877–1900
William Ivy Hair

Epidemics in Colonial America John Duffy

The First South John Richard Alden

The Earl of Louisiana A. J. Liebling

The South and the Sectional Conflict David M. Potter

And the War Came: The North and the Secession Crisis, 1860–1881
Kenneth M. Stampp

Twelve Years a Slave Solomon Northup. Edited by Sue Eakin and
Joseph Logsdon

The Suppression of the African Slave Trade W. E. B. Du Bois

F. D. R. and the South Frank Freidel

Reconstruction in Retrospect: Views from the Turn of the Century
Edited by Richard N. Current

Reconstruction: An Anthology of Revisionist Writings Edited by
Kenneth M. Stampp and Leon Litwack

Reconstruction in Mississippi James W. Garner

Origins of Class Struggle in Louisiana Roger W. Shugg

The Slave Economy of the Old South: Selected Essays in Economic
and Social History Ulrich Bonnell Phillips. Edited by
Eugene D. Genovese

The Burden of Southern History C. Vann Woodward

Jim Crow's Defense: Anti-Negro Thought in America, 1900–1930
I. A. Newby

Civil War in the Making, 1815–1860 Avery O. Craven

The Politics of Reconstruction, 1863–1867 David Donald

Look Away from Dixie Frank E. Smith

The Cold War: Retrospect and Prospect Frederick L. Schuman

Writing Southern History: Essays in Historiography in Honor of
Fletcher M. Green Edited by Arthur S. Link and
Rembert W. Patrick

Romanticism and Nationalism in the Old South Rollin G. Osterweis

The Mind of the Old South Clement Eaton

Pitchfork Ben Tillman Francis Butler Simkins

Hoke Smith and the Politics of the New South
Dewey W. Grantham, Jr.

Religion and the Constitution Paul G. Kauper

American Negro Slavery Ulrich Bonnell Phillips

The Meaning of Yalta: Big Three Diplomacy and the New Balance
of Power Edited by John L. Snell

Southern Legacy Hodding Carter

Edmund Ruffin, Southerner: A Study in Secession
Avery O. Craven

Romance and Realism in Southern Politics T. Harry Williams

Plato Eric Voegelin

A HISTORY OF THE SOUTH

The Southern Colonies in the Seventeenth Century, 1607–1689
Wesley Frank Craven

The South in the Revolution, 1763–1789 John Richard Alden

The South in the New Nation, 1789–1819 Thomas P. Abernethy

The Development of Southern Sectionalism, 1819–1848
Charles S. Sydnor

Origins of the New South, 1877–1913 C. Vann Woodward

The Emergence of the New South, 1913–1945 George B. Tindall